AF488273

May 19, 1932, 1 P.M., SS Bremen, NYC

When I saw His face
I knew to follow this Man
Anywhere. Forever.

Where Are You From?

Book interior and cover design Karl Moeller

ISBN-13
979-8-218-46009-9

Palatino typeface 12 point

Grateful acknowledgements to:
Buz Connor for two verses of his
"Mountain Song" in "He Sings."
Jeff Wolverton for photo and part of an email as quoted in
"How To Untangle Complex Threads."
Mayan and Richard Ward, in whose book, *Meher Baba's Trails*
"On the Way Down the Hill" first appeared

Available at
amazon.com
barnesandnoble.com
booksamillion.com

Front cover: Meher Spiritual Center
Back cover: Path to Seclusion Hill

Om Point

There is no end…
Can the beginning
be far behind?

The plan

is to go out with less
than I came in with.
Not in years or blood or pounds,
but fewer, lighter mental impressions—
slowly letting go of envy, revenge, lust and greed.
Knowing I am ever and always cared for.
Loved and loving.

Introduction

Throughout my life I have been asked, "Where are you from?"

I wrote these accounts of my life and these poems during the first eight years of living in Asheville, NC. They are chronological only according to the beginning paragraph(s) of each piece—then trickle on through some particular theme —thus bits and pieces of events may be repeated. So it goes.

—Irma Sheppard, June 13, 2024

Table of Contents

Table of Contents

Being loved by You
allays any fear

Bits of Caffeine

The first time I tasted coffee was in Bavaria in 1946, when I was about two and a half years old. I sat with my mother, father and older sister, along with other people around a large table. A huge bowl of coffee with milk and sugar sat in the center of the table. We each had a spoon with which to take coffee out of the bowl and a chunk of heavy brown bread. My mother helped me to get my spoonfuls out of the bowl. That's all I remember.

We were refugees. I was one and a half when we had fled Silesia early in 1945, taking only what we could carry—I was half of what my mother could carry. My mother, sister, paternal grandmother and I, along with other relatives and friends had boarded a train and ended up in Bavaria. My grandmother was ill and managed to slip off the train unnoticed during one stop. My father had stayed behind with the other men to form a wagon train with more of our belongings—bedding, kitchenware, tools. After months on the road, he found us in a refugee camp—a drafty castle, where we'd been ill with dysentery and scarlet fever. My mother told me years later that while I'd already been walking in Silesia, after dysentery and insufficient food in the camp, I could no longer walk. When the war was over, my father searched for his mother through the Red Cross, but found no trace of her.

By the end of the war there was a serious shortage of labor. A well-to-do Bavarian farmer, Herr Thiele, took us and several others to work on his farm in Witzelsdorf. That's where I had the coffee. Thiele was not a generous man—a coffee and bread supper for people who worked hard for him. After a short time, my father arranged for us to live across the road on Frau Heilmeier's farm—a spinster with a developmentally disabled brother. At first she said no to my father's offer of working her farm—he had children and she couldn't stand the fuss and bother of them. He assured and persuaded her that we would not bother her. We lived in her front room. It was good to be on a farm after the war, where there was food to be had—mushrooms from the cow pasture, blueberries from the woods, thistle greens cooked as spinach—supplemented by what I now call 'care packages' from Dad's brother and sisters in new York—canned chicken, coffee and sugar along with chocolate bars and hand-me-down clothes for us. Especially shoes.

Bavaria was occupied by the American army then—Germans were not allowed to have firearms. But armed gangs of German robbers scoured the countryside, survived by taking what they could and killing people. Thiele boasted in the village that the robbers should just come—he'd show them whatfor! The robbers must have heard about his boasting—they did come one night—killed Thiele and his whole family, but not the workers. Shocked the whole village. Talk of it spiraled in hushed tones from kitchen to kitchen. Hadn't died down completely before our family left for Canada.

Later in Windsor, Canada, I was given coffee along with the family and guests—my parents had no idea that children shouldn't have coffee—I only learned that from the Canadians. As teens, my sister, Ilse and I hung out in restaurants at night, with coffee (all we could afford) and friends. Always with milk and sugar. After Ilse married and moved away, I hung out at the Big Boy with my best friend, Marti, nursing coffees, now black and no sugar.

Ten years later in Ferndale, Michigan I was expecting my second child and it was difficult for me to finish one cup of coffee in the mornings. I switched to tea, with milk. After Alex was born I had coffee again, a cup a day, and if there were guests, maybe two.

Years later, in my early forties, in Tucson, Arizona I learned that I had adrenal exhaustion—caffeine was not my friend. I also learned that the acids in coffee work against most vitamins and many minerals. I cut way down on coffee and enjoyed my tea, now with cream. During Tucson's July and August monsoon, I'd still treat myself to iced decaf coffee with cream. But the energy issue dogged me—I had to limit even tea and switched to rooibos herbal tea for my daily treat.

In July 2003, at the Southern California Sahavas at Pilgrim Pines, I threw coffee into the *dhuni*. I have never missed it. I will not throw tea into the *dhuni*, but treat myself to bits of caffeine tea with rooibos and cream every morning.

Alone

I was four years old the first time I remember feeling alone, in Witzelsdorf, Bavaria with Ilse, nine, and her girlfriend. We were walking in the hilly countryside, not headed anywhere in particular. Maybe my mother had told Ilse to take me out for a while—we four lived in one room of Frau Heilmeier's farmhouse—maybe *Mutti* needed some private time.

Ilse told me to walk ahead of them, so I did. I heard them chattering and giggling about boys and the nuns at school—I had no interest in any of that, so I followed the path up a small hill. My attention was caught by a bright bird just up ahead. I knew the words for red, blue, yellow. *Rot* for the ribbon *Mutti* tied in my hair; *blau* for *Vergissmeinnicht*—forget-me-nots; *gelb* for *Gelberüben* — carrots; *grün* for *Gras*, of course; and *schwartzbraun* for *Haselnuss*—hazelnut. What color was the bird?

Weiss for the Queen Anne's lace, white lacy heads all along the path, nodding gently in the breeze. And forget-me-nots brilliant blue, like the little gems in a bracelet I dreamed of once, peeking at me now low on the ground. *Mohnbluhmen*, poppies, red, large-petalled and gloriously proud on tall stems. Cornflowers, daisies, fuschia, buttercups! My eyes took in these lovely blooms—clover, dandelions, the leafy greens everywhere and more and more and…I was so absorbed in the wonder, the heartful wonder of all the beauty before me. I breathed it all in. Blue sky brightened by white clouds. The gentle breeze riffling my hair, my cheek. And exhaled.

I just had to share my delight with Ilse and her friend. I swirled around to exclaim my joyful discoveries to them—and stood shocked—they were not there! I was alone.

Alone!

I heard some giggles and looked down the hillside—they were there, way down at the base of the hill, squinting at me and walking away! I couldn't believe it. How could they do this! Just turn and walk away from me like this!?

A scream stuck in my throat so I couldn't breathe. My legs went wobbly, but my arms shot out, shaking at them down there…and shook the scream out into the air.

Wait! Wait for me! Wait for me!! I fled down the hill as if something were after me.

They kept walking and smirking, as if they were so clever. I thought they were just mean. I pounded down the hill path and around to the left, caught up with them with my last heaving breaths. Fear falling out of my eyes.

"We just wanted to see what you would do," Ilse said.

I didn't know the words then. They come to me just now—I felt betrayed, abandoned. Hallmarks of our family.

If fishes were wishes
The sea would come true!

Full Circle at Last

The first time I saw rose petals strewn in front of people, I was four years old, in a city in Bavaria in 1948. It could have been in München. It could have been May 1st, May Day. My parents were arranging for us to emigrate to Canada, and some papers needed to be drawn up and signed in an office on the third floor of a building. It was the first time I'd ever been in such a building. A window overlooking the street drew me.

I saw, far below, a procession of priests and choirboys all in white surplices, singing in cadence with their steps. I stood fascinated, aware that most Bavarians were Catholic, while we were not—I must have heard my parents talk about this. What caught my breath and held it fast was the sight of girls, young, even my age, in pretty dresses and flower circlets in their long hair, gently tossing rose petals before a flower-bedecked cart.

A statue of Mary, Mother of God, stood on this cart. In the years we'd lived in Witzelsdorf, I'd seen the nearby roadside shrines many times—Mary alone or holding Baby Jesus. I didn't know their names then—they were not in my parents' conversation.

As I watched, spellbound at the window, I suddenly knew I was supposed to be there, sprinkling handfuls of rose petals on the road, honoring the Virgin Mary. My heart quickened. Yet the distance between the road and the third floor was too great. The distance between the Catholics and the Lutherans was greater. And the distance between where they were going and where I was headed was the greatest. Somehow I knew all this, though I had words for none of it, and said nothing to mother, father, sister.

Watching the girls strew rose petals awakened some ancient memory, for I knew too, that I had somewhere done this before. In July 1980, at the first Southern California Sahavas I attended, Barbara Roberts said something about rose petals strewn by virgins in Roman times. "Ahh," I thought. "That's when I did it—as a Vestal Virgin so long ago."

Six months later, in January 1981, I was in Meher Baba's Samadhi in Meherabad, India, with a small handful of rose petals to scatter gently over the coverlet of His marble tombstone. I knelt and bowed, placed my forehead at His feet. Full circle at last.

His Grace

Wrapped tightly as a rosebud
I send out no sultry scent.

The Sun's warmth allows me
to loosen that which encloses me.

The Sun's kiss awakens my longing
to embrace His radiant ways.

His Love unfolds the petals of my beauty,
His Grace draws forth the true scent of Being.

Change in the Air

The notes drifted toward us as we walked along the country road. We found our father settled into a grassy hollow where the road curved and we sat there with him as he played his accordion. The melody was not plaintive, no sign of sorrow or loss—but a familiar German folk song, as if of memories…of his childhood in Austria before the Great War…of receiving his first accordion…of early manhood in the Romanian army…of the waltzes he'd played at weddings and parties…of leaving home and workshop in Romania to resettle in Silesia in wartime Germany…of the horse-drawn wagon train in the last weeks of the war…of refugee life in Bavaria with just his hands, a few salvaged tools and his accordion to sustain our family. A folk song that used to be sung with everyone in a circle. The notes now drifted into the half light of dusk and faded into the meadow. We sat together in this keen quietness of mid-October. Tomorrow we were to leave this last emigration camp, take a final train to Bremerhaven, board a ship for Canada. Tomorrow he would exchange his beloved accordion for a few dollars. He would never play again…

…yet an ache stays half asleep within me to this day.

"But Mummy, He's Black!"

The first time I saw a Black man, I was four years old on the train on our way to Bremerhaven in Germany, to board the ship, Beaversbrae, headed for Quebec City, Canada. *Vati's* sisters and brother in New York must have sent him some money because we were seated in the dining car, white cloth on the tables. On all our other train trips, *Mutti* had put food together for us, like the canned chicken sent to us by our New York relatives, in what I now call our 'care packages.' They sent their children's outgrown clothes for Ilse and me, packaged foods, Hershey bars and tins of fruity hard candy, and Christmas gifts—dolls, coloring books and crayons, and more.

It was 1948 and we'd spent the year in one emigration camp after another, standing in line almost naked to be poked by doctors, standing in line with soup bowls in hand, waiting in train stations for hours in the night, train after train—I wondered how my father knew which one to step into. *Mutti* had had TB—that's why it all took so long, so many camps—they had to make sure she was clear of that.

They probably also checked into *Vati's* history during the war. Had he been in the military? No—he was exempted because his work as a wagon maker was vital to the home front. Had he been in the German National Socialist Party? No, he had some sympathies with it, but for some reason knew better than to sign in. Perhaps he also felt it unsafe to openly practice religious rites during the war, for he refuse to let me be baptized by a Lutheran pastor until the war was over. I was two then, still in babytalk. When they asked me what the Pastor had done during the baptism, I'd said, *"Der 'farrer hat gespitzed!"* The Pastor splashed (me). This babytalk cute enough to be repeated for years.

So we sat in the dining car, wearing out best clothes, me in a wine red dress with a round white collar. I'd never even been in a restaurant before. Maybe *Mutti* and Ilse neither, but *Vati* might have been. We were very excited—it was all new. I sat next to the window, swinging my legs under the table. watching the towns, the October woods, the fields stream by. *Mutti* next to me.

Suddenly a man walked up to our table, wearing a short white jacket with brass buttons, and he asked what we'd like to order. I hardly notice what he said. Just his black face and hands! *Aber Mutti, er ist schwartz!* But Mummy, he's black!

That's all I remember. She must have shushed me up, but that surprise of seeing a Black person stayed with me. I don't remember what I ate for my first meal in a dining car. I don't remember anything about that train trip except seeing a Black man for the first time in my life.

The Beaversbrae

The first time I was on a ship was in October 1948. We boarded the Beaversbrae in Bremerhaven, Germany — *Mutti, Vati,* Ilse and me. *Vati* was bunked with the other men, where he had a cot in a small room. *Mutti,* Ilse and I were bunked in the women's dorm. As far back as I could remember, I had always slept with my mother in the parlor of Frau Heilmeier's farmhouse, where we lived after the war, but now I was told I had to sleep by myself, and on a top bunk. I could see *Mutti* on her lower bunk across from mine, but that was little comfort for me. I have no idea why I'd always slept with *Mutti,* having always to grasp her hand firmly in mine before I could go to sleep. So there in the top bunk, I didn't know how to go to sleep—a problem I wrestled with into my mid-thirties.

Weki-Weki woke us all up each morning. He'd call out *"weki-weki"* over and over as he turned on the lights to awaken us, and exchanged some good-natured banter with some of the women. We dressed and went to the cafeteria for breakfast. I remember only the pyramid of oranges at the end of the counter. I took one eagerly since I'd only ever seen a rare lemon. But these oranges were thin-skinned, hard for my little fingers to peel and sour to boot. After a few days, the pyramid stayed stacked high—most of us ignored these sour-bitten oranges.

Aboard the Beaversbrae I first heard a song in English. Weki-Weki's radio often played "Goodnight Irene" and the melody stayed in my head. When the sea was rough, I was seasick and spent much of the day in bed. *Mutti* spent most days in bed, Ilse less so, and *Vati* almost never left his little cot. So when I wasn't seasick I was on my own a lot, scampering around like any kid. Sometimes the crew members tossed candy down to the open deck and we kids scrambled for it. The candies were always peppermints, so strong they hurt my mouth and I soon stopped grabbing for them. I palled around with a girl about my age. Everyday she told me that the ship would be sure to sink that day—so her mother said. It didn't occur to me to worry about that.

One morning *Mutti* told me it was my birthday and that I was now five years old. She had me count to five on my fingers—one number more than I could before. I was thrilled that it was my birthday and that I was five years old on the very same day! I was playing with the other kids on the deck later that day, when an older boy gave me a spontaneous shove as I stood at the edge of a shaft that opened to the sea below. A harrowing split second—then somehow I stretched out my left leg and made it safely to the other side of the shaft. Why would he do such a thing!? *Vati* saw it all from the railing a deck above. He thought I'd done very well and proudly told that story for years afterwards. But it was Meher Baba truly watching over me long before I knew of Him.

We were all excited when flying fish looped alongside our ship. Hanging over the ship rails, we watched them repeatedly rise, fly forward and slip back into the waves. We were even more excited when we spotted land on the western horizon. Canada! On October 28, 1948, we docked at Quebec City. I have no memory of filing off the Beaversbrae, nor of going through Customs, nor of boarding a train with our two suitcases and a wooden trunk *Vati* had made in Bavaria. It was packed full with feather comforters *Mutti* had sewn to keep us warm in the long, cold Saskatchewan winters. I'd gone with her to buy sacks of goose feathers in a nearby village. We had all sat in our room for hours, for several evenings, stripping the fluffy parts off the quills.

It took three days by train to reach Regina, Saskatchewan. We ate bread and the canned chicken *Vati's* sisters and brother had sent us in Germany. On the train, I remember lying in the luggage hammock overhead, listening to their talk until I fell asleep. I remember the cadence of the train rocketing forward, just as it had in all the trains we'd taken in Germany from one emigration camp to another. As we approached Regina, we were all dressed in our best clothes. I wore my maroon dress with a white collar that *Tante* Mila had sewn in Bavaria, and long beige knit stockings.

Mutti's older brother, *Oncle* John, met us at the Regina train station. When he was introduced to Ilse and me, Irmhild, he shook his head and said, "You'll have to change their names. Canadians! They'll break their tongues trying to say them."

Writing in the Kitchen

The first time I wrote something, or tried to write something was in *Onkel* John's farmhouse kitchen when I was five years old. In the winter of 1948-49. Mutti, Vati and I lived there all winter. At that time I spoke only German. Ilse was ten and stayed with *Onkel* John's family in Regina, so she could go to school and learn more English—she was the only one of us who knew more than two or three words. They made her sit in a third grade class for a few weeks, then moved her up to fourth grade. She was probably already way ahead in arithmetic. I don't know if she ever got to fifth grade there, because we left in April, took a train to Windsor, Ontario, where my parents' cousin, Erna, said *Vati* could find work.

Sometime in that cold Saskatchewan winter a letter had come from Germany in a blue airmail envelope. I don't remember taking the long snowy walk to the mailbox that day. Maybe *Onkel* John brought the letter to us, addressed to his house in the city. *Mutti* opened the letter in the kitchen. *Onkel* John also brought a big bag of puffed wheat, for our breakfast, he said. While he was showing me the puffed wheat and giving me my first shiny Canadian dime with a sailing ship on one side and the profile of King George VI on the other, *Mutti* came into the living room. She'd been crying. Dad and *Onkel* John shuffled around, talking about the blizzard a couple of days ago, how the black horse was doing, the chickens and their eggs. I'd found one of my cousin's old coloring books in a cupboard and some crayons—I tried to color Porky Pig, having no idea who or what it was.

Mutti kept crying after *Onkel* John left, crying as she fixed supper for us. It was dark outside now and the kitchen had the only electric light in the house—a fixture hanging from the ceiling, with a green shade below the light bulb. I didn't know why she was crying—nobody said. *Vati* got busy candling the day's eggs at the kitchen table, where the airmail envelope lay. The writing on it intrigued me. I found some paper and a pencil stub. Had I ever held a pencil before? I scrutinized the writing on the envelope —had no idea what it said—that it was a name—*Mutti's* or *Vati's*—that there was an address—*Onkel* John's—that there were numbers as well as letters—house numbers. To me, at five, it was all of a piece—perhaps the first en-velope I'd ever seen up close. *Mutti* kept her back to us.

I began to copy the first letter, the first word, the second and so on, and then the numbers—copied them all as best I could, pressing the pencil down hard on the paper. It kept me occupied. *Vati* glanced over at me from time to time, but he didn't say anything until *Mutti* said supper was ready. He gave my paper an appraising look and said *"Fein."* I knew it didn't look nearly as neat and ele-gant as the German writing on the envelope, but his *"fein"* was good enough for me. *Mutti* didn't look at my paper, at my writing. Nobody kept it, so that historic piece is lost forever.

I was fourteen when Ilse started telling me details of our family's goings-on—past and present. Among the things I learned from her was the fact that Mom had had a lover in Silesia, where we lived during the war, and where I'd been born. This was a man who loved her, wanted her to leave her husband and marry him—he would be a father to Ilse and me, he told her. It must have been enchanting to feel so loved and wanted during the war— safe despite all the moves, the hardships, the losses. But she'd said no—she couldn't take her husband's children away from him.

I think now that that was the noblest thing I ever heard from or about my mother. It occurs to me now, decades later, that she'd been thinking of her own decision to stay with her husband, when she destroyed a postcard that arrived for me at their Michigan address. It was from Victor, whom I'd met in Windsor in the winter of 1964 and whom I'd met up with again in Köln, Germany later that summer. I'd just married Cliff Sheppard in March 1965— we were living then in Mount Clemens, Michigan and expecting our first child. Dad told me a postcard had come from Alaska—I knew Victor had wanted to go there—he was quite the adventurer, the traveler. That had appealed to me, yet I knew we were not up for a serious relationship. I imagine now that she was trying to save me the grief and longing she'd experienced. But when Dad told me, I was incensed that she was once again, trying to make decisions for me that were not hers to make.

Mutti left Silesia just before the end of the war, along with the other women and children, and we ended up in a refuge camp housed in an ancient Bavarian castle. My father and the other men arrived as the war was ending. Had Mom stayed in touch with her lover? I don't know. Ilse didn't say. Ilse did say Mom got a letter from Germany while we were staying at Uncle John's farm. I don't know who wrote the letter. What it said was that Mom's lover had died. So he was gone and there was no chance of a reunion someday. Had they talked about that possibility? *...someday after the war...?* Had she held on to his love that long? Was he the precursor of the string of lovers she later had in Windsor?

That evening in Uncle John's farm kitchen, I'd watched my father pick up each egg he'd gathered that morning from the henhouse. He'd held it up to the light to see if there were any blood spots in it, if it had been fertilized by the rooster. I sat next to him, totally absorbed in copying the letters of my parents' names—trying to write for the first time in my life. And there was so much I didn't know.

A New Face in Kindergarten

The second time I felt wronged was in kindergarten, in 1949. I was five years old and we had arrived in Windsor, Ontario by train from Regina, Saskatchewan in April. Since neither of my parents spoke English, ten-year-old Ilse, must have enrolled us at Victoria public school. She'd gone to English classes in Germany when we were in various emigration camps. While I'd spent the winter with my parents on my uncle's farm, she'd stayed in town with his family in Regina so she could go to school. Many English-speaking responsibilities fell to her. At Victoria she was put into a third grade class and I into morning kindergarten. When my mother decided to get a job sewing collars onto shirts, Ilse arranged for me to go into an all-day first grade class for the last two months of the school year.

One morning before the kindergarten class actually started, I was coloring at a little table with some other children, when the girl sitting next to me spoke to me and gestured that I should follow her. She probably said something like, "Come with me." "Come" sounds like *"komm"* so I understood. No one usually spoke to me—not only was I a new face in April, but I spoke no English. So I got up and followed this girl to the large bay window. She may have said, "I want to show you something," as she pointed out the window. I looked out at the lilac bushes, the tulips, the grass, the rain, and when I turned back to her, I saw that she had run back to her seat. And another girl had taken my seat. The two of them giggling. I stood there in a bit of shock. Felt the unfairness of the trick—all of which I had no language for.

Decades later, in my forties, I related this to a therapist. She told me that the girl hadn't tricked me, that I hadn't been wronged, that I just thought of it that way. I didn't believe her.

Feeling wronged seemed to be a core issue for me in this lifetime. I have made progress in letting go of many small incidents, even the greater abuses I received in my family. I recognize the challenge is to let go of thinking I'm in the right, regardless of what happened. I ask Meher Baba to help me get to the field Rumi spoke of—beyond all ideas of wrong-doing and right-doing. To meet Him there! To want *this* is a gift. So the situations that brought me to want this must also be His gift. His Grace.

Harvest

We're all in Baba's feedlot—
He's fattening us up
growing our plummy egos
so He can pluck them off
when they're ripe
and no longer rotten.

Keeping Time

The first time I wore a watch was in the summer of 1949, when I was five years old. We had just arrived in Windsor, after spending a long winter on my uncle's farm. Dad had said he couldn't make a living in Saskatchewan, so at Mom and Dad's cousin's encouragement, we moved to Windsor. Aunt Erna said he'd find work there.

We were living in a two-room apartment on the second floor of a house on Goyeau Avenue, near downtown. Dad's older brother and two sisters drove in from New York to visit us. They hadn't seen him since he was a boy—having emigrated to the United States decades before World War II—and they were pleased and relieved that we had survived the war, though their mother had not. *Onkel* Martin, *Tante* Katie and *Tante* Pauline. After the war they had sent us clothes, food, money, treats and Christmas gifts.

They treated us here too—buying Ilse and me matching dresses, shoes and underwear, and a toy watch for me! Maybe Ilse, who was almost eleven, got a real watch—I don't remember because I was utterly thrilled with my toy watch. On *Onkel* John's farm, I had begun to learn how to tell time on the kitchen clock—and here I had my very own timepiece!

We all climbed out our second story window onto the roof of the porch below and took snapshots. I thrust out my wrist so my new watch would show up in the photo. Smiling with sweet pleasure. I looked pretty cute, with newly cut little bangs to cover my too big forehead. Mom worried that meant I was too smart and I'd have a hard time finding a man who'd want to marry me. I have no idea what happened to that toy watch.

When I was twelve, Mom and Dad gave me my first real watch for Christmas. Bulova, with a leather strap. That set the standard—all my watches then had leather straps. I liked having a watch, though I'd rather have had a poodle skirt or a girl's bike instead of the second-hand boy's bike Dad found for me. This watch was my family's signal that I was growing up. Indeed, I stood five feet, six inches, already taller than Mom, and just an inch shorter than Ilse, who probably gave them the idea that I should have a watch. I wore that watch for years and have no idea what eventually happened to it.

When I married Cliff Sheppard in March 1965, my parents, in addition to paying for my elegant ivory wool suit, knitted by the Italian women on Erie Street, a bouquet of daisies for me and yellow rose boutonnieres for everyone else, our wedding photographs, and for a superb dinner at a Hungarian Supper Club in Detroit, gave me a gold watch. Swiss. I was twenty-one, on the verge of graduating from the University of Windsor—surely grown up now. I think it also indicated that they approved of Cliff and his family, even though they were not German. I wore that watch throughout my marriage to

Cliff—at least seven years. By that time Mom had died. I don't remember what I did with that watch either.

The first watch I bought for myself was a Timex. Sturdy, serviceable. I wore it as a single working Mom, with any number of forays into the wild side, including my first trip to India and my second marriage, this time to Karl Moeller. Its itinerary with me went from Ferndale, Michigan to Athens, Greece, to a five-month camping trip across the United States, to Venice Beach, California, to Detroit, Michigan, to London, England, to Meherabad, India, to Ottawa, Ontario, to Detroit, to Norfolk, Virginia, to Tucson, Arizona. I wore it till it just wore out.

After Dad died in 1990, his wife, Luella, said I should have his gold watch. Swiss. He had wanted Alex to have it, but Alex had died in a car accident three years earlier. I took Dad's gold watch to India with me in 1991, when Stephanie and I spent two months in Meherabad. Minoo Bharucha took small busloads of us on daytrips to Upasni Maharaj's Tomb in Sakori—lunch on banana leaf plates, cross-legged on the floor, upstairs with the nuns; to the cottage where Baba and Upasni Maharaj met for the last time, and to Sai Baba's Tomb in Shirdi. Minoo had originally been with Upasni Maharaj, so he had lots of stories to tell. He was a big joker too—going on about whiskey and women…He'd have little groups of us to his room in Lower Meherabad for tea.

Once just after Silence Day, 1991, I was sitting next to him outside Baba's Room, next to His Samadhi, as we watched the long line of pilgrims waiting to enter Baba's Samadhi, to bow at His feet. The humidity of the monsoon had all but disintegrated the leather band of Dad's watch, and I was having a hard time winding it. Minoo said, "Give it to me." I did. He put it in his shirt pocket, and we continued to watch the procession. As we prepared to leave after a while, he pulled the watch out and handed it over, admonishing me, "You shouldn't give this watch to just anyone who asks for it." As if I would.

When I returned to Tucson, I got a job as a counselor at a women's residential treatment center. By that time, I'd thrown out the disintegrating leather band, planning to get a new band when I had time. In the meantime, I kept the watch in a deep pocket of my skirt. One day soon after, it disappeared. It was just gone!

Baba said that precious stones and metals retain the energy and *sanskaras* of their owners. So Dad's gold watch must have had some of his *sanskaras*, some of which were definitely unnatural. I tell myself the story that when Minoo put that watch into his pocket, that some negative *sanskaras* were cleared from it. And that the watch's later disappearance was totally for my benefit, clearing more negative energy I may have gotten from my father. I bought myself another Timex, which lasted close to twenty years.

In August 2011, our friends from Taiwan came to visit—Ben, Ching-Fen and Ru. We took them to Mt. Lemmon, to Tombstone (the town too dumb to die), to the Desert Museum and for some shopping, where I bought my last Timex. I wore it until one day I realized that there was a clock or two in almost every room in our house—that I didn't really need to wear a watch. I took it off and put it in a drawer.

In 2016 Karl and I left Tucson and drove across the country to settle in Asheville, North Carolina. My cell phone had a clock. There was a clock in almost every room in our home, and one in our Honda Element. This last Timex took up residence in my bedside table drawer, remaining content to lie there, keeping time all to itself.

in this moment

rain patters on the roof
an exuberant pine dances in the window
I am reading a lighthearted book
a cat sleeps somewhere in the house
birdsong interrupts the rainsong
a friend is coming for tea
this moment in Meher's Grace

Garbage Wasn't the Only Thing That Stank

The first time I smelled garbage was in Windsor, where we lived on Goyeau Avenue in a two-room apartment for a few months, April through June, 1949. Jimmy Okvath was our Hungarian landlord—he became a family friend for the rest of his life. His wife and children were still in Hungary and he lived in a run-down house, full of old men. Dad said he was a communist, but that didn't seem to stop them from being friends.

Mutti used to do his laundry the first few years we were in Windsor. Ilse and I would collect it in a little wagon he gave us, and later we'd walk the clean, pressed, folded clothes back to his place a few blocks away. He'd give us each a hug and a dime. On our way home we'd stop at the corner store for candy, especially chocolate bars. I don't know what *Mutti* got for her trouble.

The alley behind the house we lived in was loaded with garbage—it had its own stinky, rotty smell. On Frau Heilmeier's farm in Bavaria I'd smelled pigs, cows and cow pies, horses, rabbits and hens' nests and our out-house. Hay, buttercups, poppies and daisies. Poppy seeds, wheat in the field, fresh-shaved wood in Dad's workshop. Blueberries in the woods, Hershey chocolate bars sent by *Tanten* Pauline and Katie, *mamaliga* (corn-meal mush). Snow, ice, pine, water from the pump, woodsmoke from the castiron stove. But I'd never smelled garbage. Alleys too were new to me.

On the Bavarian farm there was almost no packaging and the pig ate almost everything else. On Uncle John's farm in Saskatchewan, it was winter—snowbanks taller than me. No alleys. Nothing stank.

It was in the alley behind Goyeau Street that I heard my first dirty jokes. It wasn't just my lack of English—I didn't understand anything except that the jokes were dirty (I learned that word) and that I was supposed to laugh. The word 'fuck' came up often enough that I knew it was intimately involved with the dirty jokes. Garbage wasn't the only thing that stank in the alley. I was fourteen before I began to understand what 'fuck' was about.

Garbage wasn't the only new smell in Canada. Bananas, ice cream, grapefruit, chewing gum (Wrigley's), licorice. And *Mutti's torten* (cakes), that she could bake for us now that she had all the flour, eggs, cream, cinnamon, vanilla, sugar and lemon she needed. And coffee to drink with the cake. Real coffee instead of *ersatz*.

Highland Avenue

I was five years old in Windsor when I had a friend for the first time in my life. From 1948 to 1949, we'd moved from a Bavarian village to my uncle's farm near Regina, to Windsor. From the two rooms we'd first rented on Goyeau Street from a Hungarian man to sharing the house of a Polish man on Highland Avenue. How did my father find these people? I could speak and understand bits of English after the three months of kindergarten and first grade classes they'd put me in from April through June. When we moved to this neighborhood on Highland Avenue everything was still new and strange to me. *Mutti* even began to talk in her old German dialect, which she'd never used with me before. She'd always spoken to me in High German. One day I had to say to Ilse, *Was hat sie gesagt?* What did she say?

The changes in my world and in my family kept coming and all I could do was to keep stepping into them. Kind of like the moving stairs we were on one time. Looking back, I see I had wrapped up some part of myself, to be kept safe as I watched everything and everyone. I'd shift between curiosity and shyness, remembering the time in the alley behind Goyeau, when Ilse and I watched some girls play with a skip rope. One on each end twirling the rope and one jumping up and down as they chanted all together. I had never seen anything like this before. I was enchanted. My mouth hung open, my eyed fixed in fascination. *What're you staring at?!* one girl yelled at me.

Shocked me out of my reverie. Ilse pulled at my hand, whispering, *Komm', komm'weg!* Let's go!

On Highland, all the kids played together—colored and white—skip rope, hopscotch, tag, hide'n'seek. I learned more bits of English—the kids were happy to teach me— they were nice to me. Play became vital in my daily life— how I learned more English, got to be with other kids, learned rules, had fun, got out of the house, used my body in all kinds of ways, grew strong and agile. It was Sherry Morgan who became my friend—first ever. Her skin was a very light brown and she had cinnamon eyes and hair. We walked to school together in September, first grade for both of us. She lived across the street from me with her younger brother, her mother and grandmother.

One time Sherry said, "D'you wanna come play in my house?" Feeling safe with her and adventurous, I nod- ded. "This is Irma, from across the street," she told her mother, a tall, handsome, dark-skinned woman, and to her grandmother, who sat quiet in a chair in the kitchen. I'd already met her little brother who had a mass of dark curly hair. In the Bavarian village where we'd been refu- gees, I was taught to curtsey to any adult I met, even if I didn't know them, and say *Grüss Gott.* (I greet God in you.) So when Sherry introduced me to her mother and grandmother, I curtseyed to them and said *Hello*, know- ing enough to not greet them in German. We played in her bedroom for a while and then it was suppertime, so I went home.

The next day as we walked to school, Sherry told me, "My Grammy says you can come visit again, 'cause you've got good manners." Decades later it dawned on me that no white girl had probably ever curtseyed to Momma or Grammy in their lives. It also took decades for me to be aware of what it meant that there was no father in their household, and how much lighter-skinned Sherry was than her mother and grandmother. She must have had a white father, but she never talked about a father. It took me that long to make sense out of what I simply accepted in my playmate and her family.

As we walked to school one time, Sherry pulled out a little roll of fruity candies that looked like tiny doughnuts. "D'you want one of these Lifesavers?" Happily I took one and popped it into my mouth. The next day when she pulled out her Lifesavers, I was all eyes and sure enough, she gave me one. But I didn't have anything to offer her. The next time she pulled out her Lifesavers, they were peppermint and she said, "I can't share these 'cause I have a sore throat and Mamma says I need to keep them all for myself." She had a good story every time after that. I was a little disappointed, but I understood. We still always walked to school together and played together.

One morning on the way to school I said, "My tummy hurts." Sherry told me, "You have a stomach aig". For years I thought I had a stomach egg. Just another of the strange things in my life that I had to accept without explanation, and the beginning of lifelong tummy problems. How to take in all these changes in my life? *Mutti* and *Vati* were too busy surviving in their ways—finding work and beginning to learn English—to give much attention to my needs beyond the basics. I was an adult before it occurred to me that Sherry meant "stomach ache." She also told me about #1 and #2—things I was never taught in a classroom, or at home.

Bonnie Patterson lived down the block—a sweet girl with a sweet smile. Skin and hair much darker than Sherry's, but her smile much brighter. I sensed that she came from a happier home than Sherry's or mine. Sometimes at recess I heard the word 'nigger,' which I knew meant something bad by *that* tone of voice and that look on the face. I never used that word. Sherry and Bonnie liked me. They walked and talked and played with me. Nothing else mattered.

For weeks, Sherry grabbed me every afternoon just after the school bell rang and urgently said, "We have to run home down the alley, so Joe can't catch us and beat us up." She was all wide-eyed, eyebrows wrinkled and raised, a catch in her voice. Joe was a couple of years older and lived on Mercer Street, behind Highland. So we'd sneak out a side door and hustle down an alley until she declared us safe for the day. It never occurred to me that I never heard Joe threaten us, nor did he chase us. So Joe Morgan never caught us. I saw him lounging on the school steps once. He said something to me, made a suggestion I didn't understand, except that by the expression on his face I knew it was not nice. Now when I think of it, my guess is that if Joe had caught us, he'd have done something other than beat us up.

Joyce Morgan was different. "We're not related," Sherry made sure to tell me. Joyce lived on the next street over, Mercer. She wasn't pretty and she scowled a lot. I saw her smile a few times, but her mood was usually so foul that I didn't trust her fleeting smiles. Unlike Sherry and Bonnie, whose hair was done in long braids and tied with ribbons, Joyce's hair was short, parted into squares, and each square of hair braided into a tiny pigtail. In class, she undid one or more of them, and rebraided them, over and over. The teachers didn't seem to mind.

I never understood why Joyce was so crabby, even mean. Her older cousin, Joe Morgan, lived on Mercer too. I never walked there—between Joyce and Joe, it felt dark and menacing to my six-year-old self. Joe and his pals hung out on the school steps outside, waiting for us girls to come out after school, so he could make smutty remarks. I didn't understand his words, but took in his tone—*dirty*—a word I'd learned in the alley behind Goyeau. It took me decades to have any idea of what was bothering Joyce so much. Or *who* was bothering her. Joe was her cousin. They lived on the same block. Maybe next door. No wonder she felt angry and helpless and mean.

The only white girl I remember from Highland was nice to me too, showed me how to play skip with a jump rope. Then Dad made me one. She invited me into her house once too. In her bedroom, she wanted to play doctor. When she showed me how, I said I didn't want to. I didn't go back.

Then there was Gerald. He lived on Highland too. One day in October, as I was walking to school by myself, Gerald came up behind me and kissed my cheek. Then he gave me a shove—not real hard— and yelled as he ran on ahead, *You better not tell!* I didn't know about 'telling' yet, or why it was so important to not tell on him. He was a nice-looking boy, medium brown, with nice eyes. Kinda shy. This was my first kiss.

Because my mother had TB again in 1950, and had to stay in the sanitorium, my sister and I were sent to stay with relatives on Long Island, New York for six months. So I was in second grade at P.S. 37 Queens there and not in Windsor. When I returned, Sherry and I were in the same class again for third grade. We still played together at recess, but we weren't best friends anymore. There was no problem between us, just that I was gone for such a long time, and we'd moved again, to Lillian Street, a few blocks away. It was never the same again.

My Unlovely Behavior

The first time I stole something was in the summer of 1949 in Windsor, when I was five years old. We were living on Highland Avenue in the home of a Polish man, who kept the back bedroom for himself, renting us the rest of the small house. That's where I continued to learn English from the kids on the block—from the games they taught me—hide'n seek (which I heard as *hinegoseek* for years), skip, tag, statues, Mother may I? They had toys—balls, skipping ropes, tricycles, baby buggies, pails and shovels and more. I had two dolls, given to me by relatives in Regina for Christmas, but I don't remember playing with those at all. Maybe I wasn't allowed to take them outside. I would have wanted to push them in a buggy like the other girls did.

One day I was alone outside and saw a toy shovel on the grass between the sidewalk and the street. All of a sudden I wanted that shovel, lusting after having a toy of my own. I looked around—nobody out at all. I edged over and sat next to the shovel, took it and concealed it under my dress. I got up, thinking to hide it somewhere and play with it. Another thought stopped me. I realized I could never explain how I got this shovel—everybody knew I didn't have anything like this. I looked around again—coast was still clear. I edged back to the spot where I'd found the shovel, and stealthily put it back.

The next thing I remember stealing was penny candy at Joe's Market. His bleachblonde cashier, Rose, never caught me. Sometimes I'd filch pennies or nickels from my parents' card playing stash—to get more candy.

As a teen, my best friend, Marti, and I would go shopping for clothes in Detroit, just across the river. Canadian dollars were worth more than American dollars then, so we'd get good deals. Sometimes we'd skip school, get our mothers to sign notes we'd written—like when teachers were doing boring reviews before exams. We'd shop downtown Detroit's Hudson's Basement, or when we old enough to drive, go to Atlantic Mills, a huge bargain outlet. I never had much money and I always wanted more clothes. I'd find a couple of things I could afford to buy and then choose something that I could easily steal. I would wear this or stuff it under my skirt belt and smuggle it back across the border. I never got caught.

My next major stealing binge was on our five-month cross-country camping trip in 1977— Donald Hill, Stephanie and I. I'd steal food from large groceries, tuck an item or two in my bag as I shopped, feeling like a smarty-pants, entitled and rationalizing that it was just from big corporations. As if I were emulating the romance of Robin Hood. When we arrived in Venice Beach, California, I continued my habit. It was when I took some coffee and chocolate from Safeway that I was caught. My eleven-year-old daughter was with me, and I was embarrassed and profoundly sad that she had to see me arrested, questioned and fingerprinted. I said to her, "Don't do this. Don't steal." (She said, "I don't.") A different message than I'd gotten from my father, who'd said to me when I was a teen, "Do what you want, just don't get caught." I pled *nolo contendere* in court and paid the sixty dollar fine.

The fingerprinting cost me an ESL teaching job a few weeks later. Teachers had to be fingerprinted and they caught up with me. In a way it was just as well—I was burned out on teaching and it was a long drive to the school, in heavy traffic, at night. This didn't stop me from stealing, though. I was defiant and just paid better attention so I wouldn't get caught. So what convinced me?

A year later, I was working as a recreation director at a board and care facility on Pico Boulevard in Santa Monica. One day in Venice, a few days before Easter 1979, I saw a pretty blue velvet pillow in a trash pile and took it for the sofa in the OT shop at work. On Saturday I brought two huge pots of boiled eggs into the OT shop for the residents to color—they would each have two Easter eggs with their breakfast the next morning. Out of breath after lugging the pots from the kitchen to the OT shop, I sat on the sofa to rest.

Irene, a resident, walked in. She had never come in before, nor gone on any of our outings in Los Angeles County, so I was surprised to see her. Irene was not easy to look at—short, dumpy, grey-white hair sticking out all over, blackheads all over her nose and face. "I want my Easter egg," she said.

"We're coloring them today." I said. "You'll get two tomorrow morning."

"I want my egg now."

"No, Irene, not until tomorrow."

She moved over to the pot on the table and I got off the sofa. If I let Irene have one now, I'd have a parade of residents wanting an egg now. When Irene saw that I'd stopped her from taking an egg, she went and flopped on the sofa. I began to color the eggs with the other residents there. Soon after, I saw Irene walking out with the blue velvet pillow!

I watched her with amazement, feeling outraged and thinking, *Who does she think she is!?! Thinks she can just take anything she wants and walk out with it!!*

Yes, it hit me then. *Oh!* That's what *I'd* been doing. My unlovely behavior and attitude reflected back to me by this unlovely Irene.

I stopped shoplifting.

A year or so later, I experienced Meher Baba's Presence in my Venice studio apartment. I took to heart what He said: "If it isn't yours, don't take it." I had the decades-long habit of picking up coins from the street, the ground, the floor, wherever. A few years ago, I recognized how this habit tended to keep my attention down to the ground or the floor, instead of up toward the sky or to those around me. I promised Baba and myself, that I would stop doing even that. And I have.

How deeply You let
me see into my own heart—
and still You love me.

His Costar

The first time I saw a movie was in Windsor in the summer of 1950, when I was six years old. Ilse and I lived in a row house next door to Sandra Allen's wartime house. Sandra, the wild girl on our block, said she'd take Ilse and me to see "Tarzan" with Johnny Weissmuller at the Park theatre. Judy Gadelovich, who lived next door to Sandra, in an identical wartime house, came with us. I mention Judy because she was one of the few older girls who was always nice to me.

Sandra said we had to sit in the front row. I don't remember why, but I was young and limber enough that I did not get a sore neck. The tickets were fifteen cents each and we got ten-cent boxes of popcorn—all new to me. I don't remember anything about the story. It was a black and white film, in which Tarzan kept company with a family of resourceful chimps.

A year later, Ilse and I were living with Pauline and Richard Benske and their son and daughter in Garden City, Long Island, because my mother was in a sanatorium with TB. Pauline was my cousin on my father's side, but older than Mom, so we called her Aunt Pauline. Richard worked at Macy's, selling TV sets, so they had three TV sets in their home in 1950!

So at the age of seven, I had regular access, just as if I were a regular American kid, to "Howdy Doody," "The

Lone Ranger," "Sid Caesar's Show of Shows," Milton Berle," "Sky King" and other kid and adult shows. When I saw a murder mystery on TV, I was surprised to see the murdered character come from behind the curtain at the end of the show and take a bow alongside the other characters—I'd believed that guy was really dead.

I liked the Lone Ranger with his white hat and black mask, and his *kemosabe* pal. They were always in the right. Buffalo Bob was a tiny tad on the smarmy side— funny that I knew that even then. I always wished I could sit in the Peanut Gallery and get the goodies they passed out at each show. Clarabelle was just goofy. I watched it all anyway. Ilse and I also sometimes went to movies by ourselves—Saturday matinees—saw "The Red Shoes," bought candy cigarettes at the confectioners' stand.

Once introduced to the world of viewing, we continued when we were back in Windsor six months later in June 1951. Early favorites were "The Magic Carpet" with Lucille Ball before she practiced making big eyes on a TV show. And "Treasure Island," which scared me, afraid for the little boy—I'd cried and cowered more than once at my mother's desperate violence by that time.

The first time I went to a movie by myself was in 1973. I was divorced, seeing this guy and that, but not for movies. My best friend in Michigan, Marty, wasn't always available either. When I wanted to see "Butch Cassidy and the Sundance Kid," I bit the bullet and went to the theater by myself. I felt awkward and self-conscious — people would see that I was alone—but I did it! Once the lights went down and the film started, I felt better, and was glad I'd come. After that I'd go see any movie I wanted, companion or no. I had plenty of practice in Venice Beach in 1979 and 1980, when Donald was too sick with emphysema to go out. By the time he'd died on the first day of spring, 1980, I was totally comfortable going to movies by myself.

These days, Karl and I rarely go out to the cinemas for movies. We choose movies from Netflix, Amazon Prime et. al. to stream on our big home screen. We set up tray tables and sit comfortably in our sitting room, eating dinner. It's easy—less expensive, no driving, no parking—less bother all around. Sometimes he makes popcorn. Sasha sits with us—lies next to me or with Karl on the love seat in his luxurious cat mode. A way different scene from sitting in the front row, watching Tarzan.

Meher Baba liked movies too. He took His *mandali* to see movies often, even sent people to go see certain films. Visited Hollywood to mingle with the stars and gave a speech on the spiritual potential of films.

I love watching films with Baba in them. I love to see His shining eyes darting from one person to another, sometimes even to me as I watch—so His spark catches inside me and I glow. His costar.

God is always in the cards

no matter what hand I'm dealt.
Sometimes He hides
behind the Kings and Queens
or pretends to be an Ace,
a Jack of all trades
or a humble three of clubs.

Hearts are trump, He says
as He plays Himself in every round
and wins my heart without a sound.

The Power of a Saint

The first time I smoked a cigarette was in 1950, when I was still six years old and Ilse was already twelve. I was with her when she stole a package of filtered Players from the drugstore. She said we had to smoke them. We shared a sofa bed, downstairs in the dining room, while Mom and Dad slept in their room upstairs. We must have had a boarder in the other upstairs bedroom. Ilse opened the dining room window and we hung out through the open curtains. She lit one cigarette for me and one for herself. She told me how to smoke it—inhale and blow out the smoke. It made me dizzy, of course, and I probably coughed a bit. Did I smoke the whole cigarette? We only did that two or three times. I rarely questioned whatever Ilse said we had to do—Mom had had her take care of me for as long as I could remember—so I was trained to do what Ilse said.

In September that year, Mom came down with TB for the second time in her life, and had to stay in a sanatorium. With Mom gone and Dad at work, Ilse said we wouldn't go to school. We stayed home and read comic books she'd got. Mom didn't let us read comic books—if she saw us with one, borrowed or bought, she'd take it away, yelling at us—someone must have told her they were bad for us. Where did Ilse get the money? Did she steal the comics too? Or did Dad give her money?

One day the truant officer knocked on our door. The eventual upshot was that Ilse and I were packed off to stay with relatives on Long Island for six months. By that time I was seven and once again in Ilse's charge on the train from Windsor to Grand Central Station in New York. The smoking stopped. The playing hooky stopped. And other stuff stopped too. For now.

When I was fourteen, Ilse at nineteen had been through the trauma mill a few times In addition to Dad's pickup truck, we now had a car, a 1952 Consul, a British Ford. It was a tiny car. One of my jokes was that if we needed more room, we'd take out the ashtray. Every night after dinner, I'd go out with Ilse, cruising. I'd be sure to have all my homework done before dinner, and off we'd go, visiting one of her girlfriends, attending church choir re-hearsals, hanging out in restaurants nursing coffees, parking at the Hi-Ho Drive-in, where I'd entertain the guys in the next car with my jokes while they kept their eyes on Ilse—a true blonde and passing for Marilyn.

When she was driving us around, she'd tell me to light up one of her menthol Cameos. I'd take a few puffs be-fore I gave it to her, and then, even though she told me she didn't want me to start smoking, I started taking one for myself. I got nauseous a couple of times, but then I was okay. Smoking. Buying my own packs. Sometimes snitching one of Dad's home-rolled when I was desper-ate. Never a heavy smoker, my max was ten cigarettes a day—that's all I could handle without feeling sick. My friend, Marti, was smoking too. Lunch hours we'd eat quickly, then hustle to the corner store, where kids hung out and we'd smoke there. Being cool. My joke then was that I was trying to stunt my growth. It didn't work.

In 1963, Mom, Dad and I immigrated to the United States. Dad got a job paying twice what he'd earned in Windsor and they bought a house in Southfield, Michigan. By this time Ilse had married and moved to Florida. I had just completed grade thirteen then, the equivalent of first year university, free but much more difficult. Desperate to stay in Windsor and go to Assumption University with Marti, I negotiated an agreement with my parents that if I got a scholarship, I could stay with family friends, who lived a mile from the university. I had to get an A in each of nine subjects—each one had a three-hour exam in May, and that's all that counted for the whole year. Numbers but no names on the exam papers, which were sent to Toronto to be graded.

I made a promise to myself and perhaps to God, that if I got the A's I needed for a scholarship, I would stop smoking. Well, I did. And I did. In the first year I lived with the Frambach family I did not smoke. What got me going again? I thought it would help with my constipation. No shit. It did help once or twice—and then the habit kicked in again. It didn't help that Rudy, Marga and Norbert also smoked, but I can't blame it on them.

Cliff, my first husband, smoked. The only time I didn't was when I was pregnant with our second child. Within an hour of his birth, I wanted a cigarette again—another missed opportunity to quit. Cliff continued to smoke, always more heavily than I did. In 2016, I saw him on his FaceBook page, sitting in a wheelchair with oxygen, looking very ill, missing teeth and much of his dark wavy hair gone. A note said he had emphysema and that he regretted not having quit smoking earlier. I'm pretty sure he has died since then. It was a shock, since he'd always been so strong and healthy.

With Donald, I let go of menthols and took up his non-filtered Camels. So cool. Now I was at a max of five a day, but was also smoking dope—holding it in, getting high—for seven years. In Venice, Donald's lifetime asthma turned into emphysema, and within a year and a half he died. He'd had to quit, but that barely slowed his illness down. How many times did I take him to Emergency at 3 or 4 A.M.? It scared me. I was the first person to touched his dead body, taking on some of his sanskaras. A month or so later, a dog in the alley looked at me for a few seconds, suddenly shivered violently, yelped, jumped straight up and sped away. Taking those sanskaras off me. I didn't understand this until years later.

I tried to mess up my habit. I'd smoke the occasional cigar. I'd pick butts off the sidewalks if they were big enough for three or four puffs. I'd roll my own. I'd stop buying packs of Camels and get just one or two cigarettes from the little shop where I worked. I got down to one cigarette a day—the one that helped me get to sleep. One day I didn't smoke at all. That night I didn't sleep at all. The next day, again I didn't smoke. That night I didn't sleep. After 3 A.M. I panicked and ran down to the liquor store and bought a pack of Camels. That really scared me—being so dependent on cigarettes.

One day, after reading *Listen, Humanity*, which I'd inherited from Donald, I experienced Meher Baba's Presence, and *knew* He was God. I went to my first Baba meeting on Friday, June 13, 1980 and I kept going. At the meetings I heard about the July 4th *Sahavas*—they'd have a *dhuni* there. I'd read about the *dhuni* in *Listen, Humanity*—I could throw into the fire something I wanted to give up. I knew I had to go to this *sahavas,* to throw smoking into the *dhuni*. It was the only way I could stop smoking. I did that. Meher Baba said that the *dhuni* has the power of a saint, and it indeed took away all desire to smoke. I never felt the urge or the need for a cigarette ever again. I am eternally grateful. My first night home after the sahavas, I didn't know how to get into bed without my bedtime smoke. I turned around and around in small circles, like a dog getting ready to lie down. It felt very strange. I think that in throwing in smoking, a lifetime of habits were shaken up, and I was disoriented—an opportunity to re-orient!

You are silent within me,
yet You let me know
what is yes
and when is no.

We Needed To Live Elsewhere

The first time I lived in the United States was in November 1950 when I was seven years old and Ilse was twelve—we took a train from Windsor to Grand Central Station in New York. My mother had tuberculosis for the second time in her life in the late summer of that year, and had to stay in a sanatorium for a year. Ilse and I started school again after Labour Day—she in seventh grade and I in second. With Mom gone, Ilse decided we would play hooky, read comic books all day, which Mom had always forbidden. After some days of this, a truant officer knocked on our door. Fortunately for us, someone decided we needed to live elsewhere, so we avoided various actual and potential abuses for the time being.

The most viable option was to live with Dad's niece, Pauline, in Garden City, Long Island. She agreed to take us in. She had two children—Richie, fourteen and June, ten. We spent countless hours of waiting in the halls of office buildings, along with Pastor Friedrichsen, who helped negotiate the paperwork permissions for us to reside temporarily in the United States, since we were not yet Canadian citizens. Finally we departed Windsor by train early in December, ate our packed lunches and that evening arrived in New York.

Pauline and her family met us at Grand Central Station and on the way to Long Island, drove by the gigantic Christmas tree in the Rockefeller Center. I was too tired, even sleepy, to appreciate its grandeur. She enrolled us in P.S. 37 Queens in our respective grades. We took a school bus each morning and afternoon, had lunch in the school cafeteria. For the first time I ate tomato soup—I never liked it, and grilled cheese sandwiches—I did like them. Every morning in class we had to write a page or so called "Daily News." Once I wrote about our cocker spaniel and her new puppies—how I'd play with them in the basement. Sometimes we would draw, but there was nothing like the subtraction we'd begun to learn in Miss Thompson's second grade class in Windsor.

The classroom was chaotic, kids milling about. The two middle-aged second grade teachers were a bit ditzy, fussing with each other about their hair and clothes. My teacher would fuss over one or other of us in a friendly way, but I don't remember that she ever taught anything. I enjoyed recess, playing hopscotch and learning new American rhymes to skip to. In the afternoon someone would come to the classroom selling cookies, whereas in Windsor I'd paid a nickel for a mid-morning half-pint bottle of milk. Sometimes I was taken up to the principal's office when she had a visitor. She proudly and fondly introduced me as "our neighbor from the North." I wondered why she picked me instead of Ilse—who'd always been the star and spokesman for our family. I was asked a few questions, given a cookie and sent back to my classroom. At Prince Edward school in Windsor, when I was sent to the principal's office it was only to get glared at and my hand strapped by Mr. Gibson—for being restless and talking, and once because the speech teacher tripped over my feet. I used to lisp.

It was in Garden City that I first saw a television. Uncle Dick sold TVs at Macy's, and they had three of them in their home. We watched "The Lone Ranger", Sid Caesar and Imogene Coca, and Ralph Bellamy in detective mysteries in the evenings. I'd lie on the carpeted floor, twisting around like a pretzel, trying to touch my feet to the back of my head. It occurred to me as an adult that I must have been a Chinese acrobat in a previous life. After school, I'd watch "Howdy Doody" and cartoons.

Christmas was a big event. June got all excited, knowing treats and surprises were in store, and Ilse and I caught some of the treat fever. Ilse, June and I each received a vanity case, red fake alligator, with our first names embossed in gold under the locks (my prized possession for years), bathrobes (my first ever) slippers, and more. Christmas Day we visited Aunt Pauline's sister, Sophie and her family in Islip, also on Long Island. Sophie's little son, Alvin, had received a wooden jigsaw puzzle of the United States. I took every chance I could to play with that puzzle, and the shapes of the states have stayed in my mind all these years. It seemed like I was always wanting, dying, to play with other kids' toys—I was mad with wanting to learn, to do, to play!

On Saturday mornings we cleaned our rooms. We girls slept upstairs—Ilse and June in the big room with slanted ceilings, and me in the area at the top of the stairs. We'd chat and giggle and listen to "Archie" on the radio as we dusted, mopped and changed the sheets on our beds. The kids at school were nice to me—some lived in my neighborhood, so we'd play there too. Saturday afternoons we'd beg potatoes from our Moms and roast them in a fire in an empty lot, eat them with a bit of salt, even the blackened crusty skins.

That winter I got the mumps, and Ilse, ever eager to miss school, stayed close to me on purpose, and to Aunt Pauline's disgust, got the mumps too. I was not in the habit of brushing my teeth, though I had a toothbrush. Mom never told me to brush my teeth and Aunt Pauline probably assumed that I knew to brush them. I'd been told in first grade to brush, but no one ever reminded me or made me, so I didn't. I started getting toothaches and loose teeth—I was seven—that's when we lose baby teeth. Groaning and moaning, Aunt Pauline took me to the dentist. I was a trial for Aunt Pauline in one other way—I didn't know how to wash my hands properly—no one ever taught me. We each had our own towel in the bathroom. I would wet my hands, maybe use a bit of soap and dry them on my towel, which then got dirty from half washed hands. She'd complain at me. I'd be puzzled and try a little harder so she wouldn't complain, but it was never good enough. She didn't show me how to wash my hands either, assuming that I knew how, and was just too lazy or stubborn to do it.

Another thing I didn't know how to do was how to go to sleep. I'd lie awake making up stories to amuse myself, tongue my latest loose or sore tooth, tunnel under the blankets, and so on. In Bavaria I'd slept with my mother, insisting on keeping hold of her hand before I could sleep. In Windsor I'd slept with Ilse. We'd tell each other stories, but she always fell asleep before I did. I was in my mid-thirties before I learned how to go to sleep. Too much stress and trauma in the family!

Sometime in March, June started telling us what we'd get for Easter, getting us all excited again. I remembered Easter on the Bavarian farm when I was four, finding colored eggs in a nest of small rocks in the little garden beside the house, after a tipoff from Ilse. At Aunt Pauline's, we each received a large basket filled with colored eggs, chocolate eggs, chocolate bunnies, candy, sets of matching sock and underwear and more—loot galore! Easter dresses and bonnets, a pocketbook (purse), church and an Easter Parade! Where was Jesus in all this?

For Mother's Day, Aunt Pauline took Ilse and me to a photographer's studio and had a portrait of us taken there. We wore the new dresses she'd bought us. My hair had been curled and pinned back with pink cowboy hat barrettes. This photo is proof that I had once been cute. It was around that time that I remember looking into a mirror one day, with the idea that I was beautiful. I kept looking and looking at my face in the mirror, looking for the beauty. We also each had to embroider a handkerchief to send to Mom. I stitched "Happy Mother's Day" in red embroidery floss onto the corner of a lacy white handkerchief. We wrote letters to Mom too. That was hard—I didn't know what to write that would make her feel happy—I didn't want her to think I was happier with Aunt Pauline than with her.

It was odd, living with a different family. Things had been odd for me ever since I could remember, and before that too—leaving the home I was born to, staying in a refugee camp, being ill there with dysenter. I remember leaving the Bavarian farm, staying in immigration camps, taking a ship across the Atlantic, a train across Canada, staying in Uncle John's farm, taking a train to Windsor, not speaking English, living in three different houses in one year, Mom gone, smoking cigarettes, playing hooky with Ilse, taking a train to New York. Life with Aunt Pauline was much more normal, and that was good.

Dad's sisters, Katie and Pauline, and his brother, Martin, were all very kind and generous with us. (I'm guessing that Dad sent money to Aunt Pauline toward our upkeep.) But I knew that I was not in the family, like Richie and June were. They went to different schools than ours. June had Saturday roller skating lessons, with her own skates in a little suitcase with travel stickers on it. Ilse must have remembered that—for my ninth birthday, she arranged a party and got money from Mom for a pair of roller skates for me. I loved them, even though I left a ton of skin on the sidewalks and street as I learned how to skate. It was very generous of Pauline and Dick to take us in for six months, and I believe they did everything they could to make us feel welcome and comfortable.

Late in June, Ilse and I took a train back home to Windsor, to Mom, Dad and the neighbourhood kids. I was aware that I could choose whether to talk like the Long Island kids, or I could go back to talking like the Windsor kids. To be different or to assimilate? Safer to assimilate.

When we told Mom all about our life on Long Island, she cried, felt bad that we'd had so much there, and she and Dad had much less to give us. In a rush of generosity, she promised many things. In that generous moment I asked if we could have a TV, a colored TV. For a very short time, life with Mom and Dad promised roses.

Some Poems

like so many empty boxes
after the Christmas tree spree,
litter my books.

A few still hold heat,
something given and taken
heart to heart.

My Real Mother

I don't love you any more.

She said it in English, not German. We'd been separated for a year—she with English speakers in a sanatorium for TB, and Ilse and I with relatives on Long Island, New York. Now in August, we'd been living together again for two months. Why had my mother said that to me?

Ilse must have told her that I told our Canadian friend Doris that yesterday Mom had locked herself in her bedroom, threatening to throw herself into the Detroit River. Dad tapping at her door, calling her pet names, gently telling her to open the door. I had no idea what that was all about—seven years later, Ilse told me. Of course she would know all about it.

Ilse and I were packed off to spend the day with Doris, nineteen and newly married to Dad's Ukrainian co-worker, Eric—I liked her very much. I kept waiting for Ilse to say something about what was happening at home, but she didn't breathe a word. We helped Doris make a mince pie and in the late afternoon sat together on a swing seat outside. Maybe it was the soothing rhythm, rocking back and forth, that pulled this singsong chant out of me: "I've got a se-cret…I've got a se-cret…"

Of course Doris asked, "What is your secret, Irma?" I said the bit that I knew. I was seven and knew only this tip of the family iceberg. Ilse rushed us off home a minute later.

It was the next day that Mom cornered me accusingly, as if I'd done the worst thing in the world. *I don't love you any more.* I felt I'd been bowled over backward through outer space. No words. Just alone. Floating in nowhere.

How could she say that to me? Decades later as an adult, I recognized that it was a very young part of my mother speaking then—very afraid of what I'd let slip, afraid of the family secrets being broadcast. She had to shut me up. Her skills were limited—harshness and violence from her mother and siblings instead of warm understanding.

What her statement confirmed forevermore was a separation between us. I believed her. She didn't love me anymore. Since Ilse and I had returned from Long Island, Mom had already been violent with us. For things we had not done. That served too to keep me away from her as much as possible. I began to not talk to her, except for the ordinary, the necessary bits. I kept my self to myself. Away from her. I didn't trust her anymore.

Eventually I recognized that in the moment of her statement, Meher Baba had turned a page. She still gave me food, but He was my Real Mother.

I come closer to You—
See more and more how You Love me.
I live for Your Love!

Taking a Stand: Naming

Ilse and I were playing with some neighborhood kids in the huge backyard of our row house in Windsor. I remember running into our kitchen two or three times and coming out each time with a slab of dark bread, with butter and jam. Maybe they had to wait for me as we played skip or hopscotch and got impatient. I was eight, growing a lot, and must have been ravenous that day. They teased me, chanting "Chichi garbage-bone picker..." adding to it--on and on, till it was a long string of fun for themselves. What stuck was Ilse calling me Chichi. I hated it and wouldn't answer. Begged Mom one day in the kitchen to make her stop. But I ran into a stone wall. What I didn't know then was their hushhush secret—now Mom let Ilse be the boss of just about anything, including me. After a while I gave up, let her call me Chichi, which she eventually shortened to Cheech.

I was fifteen when I met Marti at the new high school in our part of town. We became best friends and she also came to call me Cheech. No one else was ever allowed to call me that. I spent a summer in Europe when I was twenty, and Marti joined me for the second half of it. We were chatting with a couple of handsome guys in Rome when Marti casually referred to me as Cheech.

Nicolo and Alessandro looked at her and said, "What did you call her?" "Cheech. It's short for Chichi." The two looked at each other, and by the way they then looked at me, I knew I'd had enough of Chichi forever. When we were alone, I told Marti, "*Never* call me that again." She understood.

A few months later, when I was on the verge of twenty-one, Ilse and her children were up from Florida, on their annual visit with Mom and Dad in Michigan. I was in my senior year at the University of Windsor and came to visit on the weekends. We were in the kitchen one afternoon, Ilse and I at the table, when she said something to me addressing me as Cheech.

Looking at her very intently, I said emphatically, "My name is Irma." Mom stood at the sink, saying nothing. Ilse sprang up from her seat, ran down the hall to the bathroom, sobbing as if her heart were breaking.

Lament

Your name silent within me
dry as autumn leaves
blown to scatter and drift—
I long for the fullness
of Your gaze upon me
to warm my every part
and most especially my heart

Slow Learner

"Irma, go stand in the corner!"

Maybe I was surprised and embarrassed the first time, the second time, even the third, but it had become such a routine that I just got up and put my face into the front, right-side corner of the classroom. At least it was change from the hard wooden desk. Chalkboard at my left cheek and the smell of chalkdust. It was always the same. Miss McKinley, grey hair in a low bun, black, thick-heeled shoes, heavy in a navy print dress. Did she just not like me? Because I was German? An immigrant?

She'd given us some work to do—maybe a page of multiplication problems—third grade stuff. I did them. I checked them. I was done. I saw kids still bent over their papers. I pulled out my Reader and reread my favorite stories—Aladdin and his magic lamp, King Alfred burning his bannocks, the mountain with the stone face…I read a few more…looked around the room…clouds in the sky out the second floor window …kids busy with their pencils and erasers…skritch, skritch.

I wiggled my toes, my feet, my shoulders. Squirmed. Looked at the problems again. Drummed fingers on my Reader, put it back in my desk.

Manfred, German like me, sat behind me, and Herbert next to him, also German. I didn't like them much and they didn't like me much either. But I was desperate enough to twist around, guessing Manfred had finished his problems too, and sure enough, he was sketching a fleet of airplanes on a blank page. Herbert too. Not very interested, I watched. Then Manfred said something stupid about me to Herbert and they chortled. That was when Miss McKinley barked at me to stand in the corner. There was no use in telling her I hadn't said a word.

Standing in the corner, I plotted recess revenge on those bratty boys when the bell rang. That meant the upper grades were changing classes now, filing up and down the halls. The top half of classroom doors were glass, so people could see in. Ilse in eighth grade liked to check on me, and she must have done it this time too.

Mom must have had a good day while we were in school because she asked me in a benign and bemused tone, in English, "Irma, do you stand in the corner every day?" I saw Ilse hanging nearby. Without thinking I said, "No Mom. There are days when I don't." She found this very amusing, a cute story to entertain friends.

Considering how often I stood in the corner in third grade (but never once in any other grade!) I guess I was a slow learner. What could I have done differently—draw airplanes? What about Miss McKinley? Did it never occur to her to give me more problems to solve? Or to give me another book to read? So if I was a slow learner, what did that say about her?

Free as a bird

we say.
Yet birds are not so free,
but confined to feathers,
to the patterns they fly.
Solo or in formation,
they are placed into their
particular bird space.

What Is the Whole Truth?

The first time I testified in a courtroom was in the fall of 1952 in Windsor, when I was eight years old. I was testifying against John, an old man who lived down and across the alley from us. I've written the details in a short story, *The Human Touch: A Triptych*, so I'll just say that I was the youngest of four girls in the neighborhood, who let John feel them up in exchange for quarters—he patted us down over our clothes. I did it because I just wanted to be in with the older kids. When we had enough money saved up we rented bicycles one Saturday. The father of one of the girls was a policeman and demanded to know where she got the money to rent a bicycle. It all came out and he pressed charges, and we had to testify.

I felt so guilty because we had started it, knocked at John's door and presented ourselves. It wasn't until I told all this to a therapist in 1989 in Tucson, that I understood. She said John should have chased us away, closed his door—he was the adult and the responsible one. True, even though the older girls knew he was a 'dirty old man' and susceptible to our offer. John went to jail for a year. When he got out, his housekeeper made sure no girls ever entered his yard.

It took another ten years, in 1999, before I 'heard' the silence in my family about that incident. Mom and Ilse had sat silent with me in the courthouse waiting room. Even though I'd hung out with kids my mother had forbidden me to play with, no one yelled at me, accused me or slapped me for being involved in this. Nor did anyone sympathize with me. *Dead silence. Frozen.* It took decades, before I finally understood how my escapade had terrified my family—to know that child molesters could be sent to jail. Some time after that my mother started to slap me or hit me with wooden spoons when I'd said anything she called *frech*—insolent, cheeky—too close to the truth. Desperate to shut me up.

The second time I was in a small claims court in Michigan in 1972. I'd been collecting rent from Dad's tenants in Southfield, while Dad was living with Ilse in Florida. (Mom had died of an overdose.) The renters had trashed the place and I tried to get recompense. The judge said I should have gotten formal estimates of the damages, so once again I felt guilty. He still awarded me three hundred dollars for damages, but it was up to me to collect. When I knocked on the renters' back door, their German shepherd ran up and bit my leg. I didn't get to see them. They disappeared and that was that.

The last time I testified in court was in 1993 in Tucson on behalf of a client, a young woman in recovery at the residential treatment center where I worked. She wanted to regain custody of her two young children. She'd made decent progress in recent months, so I gave testimony supportive of her cause. She did regain custody of her children, and a few months later I attended her church wedding. Within a year I heard that she'd blown it all again—children, marriage, recovery. I felt sad.

The third time I testified in court in 1990 in Michigan meant the most to me. My former husband, Cliff, had filed a wrongful death suit against the man who had caused our son, Alex's death. I had not wanted to participate in this lawsuit, but was encouraged by my therapist to do so. My testimony was to show that as Alex's mother, I had had an ongoing relationship with him, even though he had not lived with me in his last ten years. I brought photographs showing he had visited me in Norfolk, VA, in Tucson, AZ and in Clawson, MI, that he had introduced me to his girlfriend and his guy friends, that we had had outings and activities together.

Before I testified, Cliff had a Michigan family state that Alex told them his mother was dead. In the witness box, I stated that Alex had introduced me to his closest friends, but had not told me anything about this family. In Cliff's testimony, he said some things that were not true. I was shocked and wanted to jump up and say so, but realized that I would then look worse. It had never occurred to me to get a lawyer for this hearing. The judge awarded the wrongful death monies to Cliff, Stephanie, her half-sister and me—I received the smallest, which in my eyes, was still considerable. We left the courthouse with Stephanie and Catherine, Cliff's stepmother.

I hope I never have to sit in a courtroom ever again.

Long for praise no longer to matter—
For stillness to please and fill the heart.

A Lifetime of Dances

I was nine the first time I danced. Every Saturday in our early years in Windsor we dressed up in our best clothes and drove to Saxon Hall for the dances there. Dad took us in his 1951 Ford pickup. Ilse sat in the middle and I had to balance myself on Mom's lap because I was the youngest and smallest. That's how we got around. Saxon Hall dances were a way to meet and connect with other German immigrants. A way for Dad to find work, for Mom to socialize, and maybe for Ilse to meet young man.

I was eight when we started to go there. I'd run around with the other little kids, drinking 7-UP and chasing through the dancers on the floor, making sure to not crash into any of them. A game we played. One evening, watching Dad dance with Mom, then with Ilse, I got the sudden idea I wanted to dance too. I asked Dad to dance with me. To show me how. And he did. The next dance was a foxtrot—I didn't know that word yet, though I knew waltzes and polkas—everyone knew those.

I stepped onto the dance floor. Place my left hand on Dad's right arm, and my right hand on his upheld left hand. As the music started, he told me to follow his steps. I promptly stepped on his shoe, but keeping my eyes glued to his feet, I got the hang of it after a minute or two. Not exactly graceful, but I'd heard the music often enough that my body fell in sync with it. We got through that well enough. In fact I felt a flush of pride and accomplishment.

I don't remember dancing with Dad there again. Ilse must have taken over—taught me how to tango, waltz and polka. She showed me how to turn my head back and forth according to the step in the waltz—said it was a more elegant way to dance. When I was fourteen she taught me how to jitterbug,—a lot more fun than the goofy shuffle I did with the other eighth graders to Elvis.

By the time I was fifteen, Ilse would take me to Teutonia, the new German club on Saturday nights. I was already taller than she was, so men would ask me to dance and that's how I learned more dance steps. One time a man, maybe Czech, who was a bit short came to ask me to dance to a samba. I started to say no, because I'd feel embarrassed being so tall. But Ilse nudged me under the table and said to me in German, "Go, he's a good dancer." So I did. And he was a good dancer. Also very kind. When I stepped on his feet, he apologized. So then I knew how to samba.

By the time I was seventeen, I was going to Teutonia with my friend, Marti (Maruta), who was Latvian. I was eighteen when I met Alfredo there for the first time and vowed to dance with no one but him. Soon after, Marti and I headed for the Italian Club, Caboto, and left Teutonia behind. Livelier Latin music and dances. I danced only with Alfredo for two years. Then we each married someone else. That story is written elsewhere.

My first husband, Cliff, and I joined a folk dancing group in Detroit. We danced in lines, in pairs, in fours. We stepped high to music from Bulgaria, Greece, Israel, Germany, Russia, Yugoslavia, Lebanon, Serbia and more. When we divorced, my participation waned. Marty (Martha), my best friend in Michigan, and I went to the Wayne State folk dance group for a while. But the way Marty put it was, "I like to dance to the music—I just don't want to learn their steps. I find my own steps." I couldn't argue with that declaration of creativity and independence, so we ended up just going to their parties and dancing there.

Marty and I would go to bars where there was good music and we'd dance with men there. She was a singular dancer. Once she got on the dance floor and guys saw what she did, they'd get in line to dance with her. I watched her too, and learned to move more than my feet.

Once, in the summer of 1975, I couldn't resist joining a line dance to "Zorba, the Greek" at a café in Athens.

I left Michigan in June 1977, camped across the country for five months ended up living in Venice Beach for three years, travelled to India and Canada for five months and ended up in Michigan again for the summer of 1981.

While I stayed at my friend, Norm's house in Detroit, I also spent time with Dad and his wife, Luella.

Once I went with them to a seniors event of music and dancing. When the band started up a waltz, Dad said to me, "Let's dance." I hadn't danced with him in decades—I couldn't remember when I'd last danced with him—maybe at Cliff's and my wedding dinner in a Detroit Hungarian Supper Club. Though for some reason I felt reluctant to dance with Dad, out of kindness or respect, I did rise and follow him to the dance floor.

We waltzed. Out of habit, I turned my head this way and that as we circled around. He told me to stop it, that it didn't look nice. He was always in tune with his idea of what looked good and what didn't. I could just as easily have stopped turning my head, but strangely, my head kept turning, until he was fed up and said he didn't want to go on dancing with me. We sat down. Somehow this was a small victory for me— the end of something.

You

are silent within me
yet You let me know
what is yes
and when is no.

Musical Posts

"I'll be keeping an eye on you," she said, looking at me with two very narrow eyes. The sharp tone of her voice added grit to her threat—'cause that's what it was. She was the principal and felt she had to keep order, and I had been out of order.

We were playing our version of musical chairs at recess, using the poles or posts that supported the portico roof by the back door of the school as 'chairs.' Four of us seventh grade kids were playing—I got into the game—wanting to win like always—I made a yowling mad dash for the post by the door—but overreached and crashed into the glass pane of the door. My arm was cut and bleeding and someone had to take me to the hospital for stitches—the first in my 12-year-old life.

It was the next day that Mrs. Judge—yes, her real name—lectured us like that—she wasn't going to stand for any more of this unladylike behavior. I didn't care too much about having her approval, but felt bad that my 7th grade teacher, Mrs. Lewis, looked equally askance at my behavior. I really wanted her to like me, to approve of me.

It was years before I understood where that excess of energy and excitement had come from. I wasn't usually so explosively loud and reckless. No. It sometimes came out at recess, at play—safe places to express whatever was bottled up inside me. Stuff from home, as usual—Mom,

Dad, Ilse—their crazy stuff that I didn't even yet know about consciously, but in some way knew something and felt the disturbed energy that made for a desperate craziness inside me sometimes… then it came out that time playing musical posts at recess.

If Mrs. Judge had known that, would she have spoken more kindly to me? Probably not. She would have shuddered inwardly, stiffened her upper lip and judged me anyway. I don't think she was a people person—not like the gentle principal at P.S. 37 Queens, New York, where Ilse and I went for 6 months when I was seven. Whenever that principal had a visitor, she would send for me and introduce me as "our neighbor from the North." Canada, she meant. And give me a cookie. A different way of keeping he eye on me. Come to think of it, Mr. Gibson, principal of Prince Edward school, used to keep an eye on me too, when we were lined up outside, ready to march in to our classrooms. He'd catch me talking or turning around and wham! he'd smack my bottom.

It was all discipline and looking good in Windsor—just like in my family. I have an inch long scar on the inside of my right arm—a souvenir—to remember it by—but it's all healed now. All of it.

My Heart
longs to be brilliant
like a diamond in the eye,
but softer

How To Untangle Complex Threads?

The first time I heard the word *nazi* was in 1956—I was thirteen in eighth grade at John Ross in Windsor. One day well into the school year, Wayne turned around in his seat at the front of the classroom, and hissed at me, *nazi*! I didn't know what it meant, but I got the message. Shocked and surprised, I was totally taken aback.

Red-haired and runty, Wayne was forever getting chased by girls around the schoolyard at recess for some cheeky, if not shitty, thing he'd said or done. Freckle-faced and mouthy, Wayne threw around words about Thursday being "fairy day" and watch out if you wear pink or purple on those days. I had no idea what he was talking about. It wasn't until I was at Assumption University years later that I understood that he and Malcolm, my brother-in-law's brother, were gay. At thirteen I had no inkling of homosexuality.

According to Wayne, I was a *nazi*, so that opened a new window into a room already full of dubious identity. I don't remember how I found out what it referred to. It was not a word used in my family or even among our German friends. I was probably in tenth grade when I found *The Diary of Anne Frank* in our school library—that opened further vistas to my possible heritage, and many questions of self-identity. And an added layer of self-consciousness. With a name like Irmhild Hexel.

Wayne's taunt was the only one I ever received on that note. Eventually I realized I was not a *nazi*. My parents had not been members of the *Nationalsozialist Partei* and my father had never been in the German military, but he did express verbal support for Hitler. I didn't know how to untangle the complex threads of those implications. With all the multiple abuses and dysfunction in my family, I knew not to ask them—I already knew not to trust what they would say.

The word *nazi* is often used as a pejorative—somewhat similar to wop, spic, kraut, wog, beaner, nigger, kike, spook, gook, commie, camel jockey, bleeding heart, red, pollack, tree hugger, junkie, pinko, trailer trash, woo woo, DP, brown nose, yellow belly, tattle tale, goon, raghead…you can add to the list.

Who has not engaged in murder, plunder, rape and genocide? The British? The Russians? The Japanese? The French, Spanish, Greeks, Romans, Egyptians, Vikings, Huns, Chinese, Israelis, Americans, Hutus, Dutch, Mongols, Persians, Canadians, Turks, Australians? Any of the so-called good guys? For over seventy years now, in film and print, Germans as *nazis* have been convenient bad guys.

Where does it begin? Where does it end?

From an email from Jeff Wolverton:

"A woman from Colorado, who had not heard of Meher Baba, one night had a past life recollection of being the victim of the Holocaust. She was trapped along with many others in a gas chamber in a concentration camp. As they were being gassed to death, she saw first-hand the scene of people on their knees praying, screaming and in terrible states of distress. However, as their bodies died, the entire group was lifted up out of that horrendous setting and was transported far away to a lovely hillside with a few buildings, a place with a most heavenly atmosphere. From above, they could hear the exquisite sound of chanting—beautiful and deep singing that soothed and transformed their subtle hearts—coming from one of the buildings below. As their hearts were transformed, they were able to leave the earth-plane and move on to the next phase of their afterlife.

A year or so later, this woman heard of Meher Baba, and someone encouraged her to go to India. When she arrived in Meherabad, she checked in at the Pilgrim Center. As she walked up the hill to Baba's Samadhi, she suddenly recognized that this was the very hillside that she and the others had been brought to after dying in the gas chambers! As it happened, this was on one of the days when the women *mandali* from Meherazad had come to pay their respects to Baba in the Tomb, which they usually did every two weeks. As the woman approached Baba's Tomb, that same heavenly chant that she had heard after coming from the concentration camp was being sung—"The Seven Names of God," composed by Baba.

During the period of the Holocaust (in the late 1930s into the mid-1940s), the women *mandali,* who were then living in the Tank building on Meherabad Hill, were ordered by Baba to spend half an hour every morning and every evening, chanting "The Seven Names of God." In later years, Eruch, Baba's close *mandali,* used to say in Mandali Hall, Meherazad, that he felt that seventy percent of Baba's Western lovers had come through the concentration camps.

The experience of this woman was further corroborated by the following: In recent years, a woman guest staying at the Meher Spiritual Center in Myrtle Beach, shared that she had heard Mehera once say that all of the victims of the Holocaust had come (in Mehera's words), "through the upper room." I (Jeff) assumed that Baba must have told Mehera this, because she usually never made such a remark on her own. This woman had naturally thought that Mehera was referring to the upper room of the main house at Meherazad, which is where Baba stayed at night. But in researching this, I found that Baba did not stay in that room until the mid-1940s. Mehera must have been referring to the upper room above the converted water tower on the hill at Meherabad. It was here during the war years that the Westeren women *mandali* were living, while the Eastern women stayed in the room directly below."

My own (Irma's) non-ordinary dream: "My daughter and I are caught. She sits upright beside me. I do not look at her. They are going to shoot us. I don't know why we are here. But they have the guns, the power. We look straight ahead. They talk and move around behind us. I hear a shot, feel her slump. She is gone. I'm next. I sense the revolver, cold, at the back of my neck. I think about the impact of a bullet entering me, and wonder that I am not afraid. Without forethought I say, *Meher Baba, Meher Baba, Meher Baba…*" I awaken, feel myself rushing back into my body.

I was born in 1943 in Krenau, Germany, twenty miles from Auschwitz. I tell myself that I died in that war and was born in that war. It is possible that I was one of those who were lifted and transported through the upper room at Meherabad Hill.

My guess is that I will continue to hear the word *nazi* used with anger, hatred, disdain, for the rest of my life. While I deeply deplore the grief and destruction carried out by the Nazis, to me that word seems often to be used like another "n" word. The challenge for me is to not react to it.

As with everything, Meher Baba conducted World War II from first to last. Who can comprehend the depth of His intentions? Just a fraction of its events and outcomes are obvious to the human eye. Judgments about who were the perpetrators and who were the victims, or who lost and who benefitted cannot be gauged by the usual standards. Underlying causes and outcomes are many-layered. And since He was and is the Conductor of it all, every person and every country and every region had to have benefitted in some way, regardless of any and all apparent losses.

Content to be at the mercy
of Your Grace, I do my best
to please You.

The Pear Tree

Late in September, about a month before I turned fourteen, Dad showed up at Patterson Collegiate, where I was in ninth grade. Three-thirty-eight in the afternoon by the time I came out of the double-doors and saw his light blue '53 Ford pick-up parked at the curb. I got in, found my old jeans and running shoes on the seat. "You can put them on when we get there," Dad told me in German, as he turned on the ignition. "There's a pear tree on the farm where I'm working. The pears are ripe now. They say we can have them all. You pick them while I finish working." He was putting imitation brick siding on the farmhouse.

We had just over two hours of daylight left by the time we got there. Biggest pear tree I'd ever seen. Huge branches splayed every which way. Easy to climb. And fun! The tomboy in me gloried in clambering from limb to limb. I filled a cloth bag over and over, took it down, emptied the pears carefully into a bushel basket. Ate just one. Picked and climbed way into dusk. A meditation—silent, fulfilling. Picked every last pear, clear to the treetop. Showed Dad. *"Fein,"* he said, *"fein."* It meant he was pleased. I could be proud. We drove home, quiet in the dark, too tired to talk. Hungry. Satisfied.

Taking a Stand

Fifteen and I make a half-smart comment,
some half-sharp observation too close for comfort.
See Mom reach into a kitchen drawer
pull out a long wooden spoon, thunder across her brow.

Sometimes she just yells, spraying images of me
tumbling backward, blood spurting on the walls.
Her nerves are flayed—too many secrets in her belly—
Dad messing with girls, her own string of lovers.

But what has that to do with me? Repulsed
at memories of being whacked by her incontinent fury,
I skip from hall to living room—she booming after—
Ich warne dich! I have never run before. Through

dining room, kitchen again. Round and round. Puffing,
short, fat, muddling behind me. How undignified for her
to chase me with a spoon. Undignified too, for me to run.
I turn abruptly, bring her to a startled halt.

Five inches taller, I face her.
Don't you dare hit me, I say in a low, even tone.
It takes a fiery moment, me staring space between us

before she lowers the spoon. In the dead silence I turn
again. My heart light as armfuls of sunshine, I walk
out of the kitchen in a snap-your-fingers kind of way.

The Japanese Landscaper

The first time I met a Japanese person was in the spring of 1958, when a tall young Japanese man came through our neighborhood and stopped at our house. In 1953 my father had bought two lots in the Windsor suburb of Sandwich East, and began to dig the basement of our house by hand. He was near fifty years old then. He framed the house, added walls and roof, had people do the plumbing and wiring, and in the spring of 1954, when I was ten, we moved in. Raw wood floors, unplastered walls inside, tar-papered on the outside—but shelter, with no rent to pay.

It took a few years for us to have the inside walls plastered and painted, imitation brick put up on the outside walls, linoleum laid down on the floors, and a cement front porch with steps put in place. Well before those, Mom and Dad put in a huge garden—almost the whole back yard—tomatoes, onions, garlic, lettuce, parsley, beans, corn, cucumbers, cabbages and a big plot of strawberries at the side of the house. Money was always squeaky tight, but we ate well, probably better than most. Eventually there was a bit of back yard grass, but the front yard sat homely in dirt and not much else.

The Japanese man told my mother he was a landscape designer, that he'd be pleased to sketch out a plan for our front yard. She put him off, saying her husband wasn't home and wouldn't be home till well after dark. The young man said that would be fine, he'd come back, say, at eight o'clock. He was very polite. She gave up and nodded, thinking my father would make short shrift of this strange-looking young man.

As many Germans of that time, my parents were proud to say we were one hundred percent German. In later years I wondered if that hadn't been a safe and convenient thing to say of oneself in Germany during the war years. It may be true though, too. As a German, my father had unequivocal views of others. Jews and churches, ours or any other, were after money and not to be trusted, yet he liked certain Jewish people very much. Russians, communists anyway, he wanted nothing to do with, but he did work for a Russian man. Italians were useless cowards—thank Mussolini for that. Ukrainians he liked and some were of his closest friends. Poles, Czechs, Slavs, Hungarians were all okay—just keep an eye on them—certain Germans too.

So by eight o'clock Dad had had his supper and the Japanese came—tall and slender but unlike any European. How would this go? I stuck around to listen. They sat at the kitchen table and looked at the sketches the landscape designer had brought. A hedge between the driveway and a lawn, flowerbeds, shrubs and a maple tree in the middle of the lawn, maybe a few more details. Dad looked at it closely, asked how long it would take. He liked things to be wrapped up quickly.

Dad always enjoyed meeting people from other places, other cultures, trading stories. He could get on in six languages. He asked the Japanese landscaper where he grew up, his parents? They'd come before the war, when he was a small boy. Vancouver, then to relatives in Windsor. It echoed some of our story—we had landed in Quebec City, took a train to Saskatchewan, and after one winter there, took a train to Windsor. In broken but confident English Dad outlined his journey from Austria to Romania to Silesia to Bavaria to Canada, the wars in between. The young man listened closely, blinked and nodded with understanding. His parents were immigrants too.

Dad drummed his fingers on the table, put a finger on the sketched out flowerbeds and said his wife would do those. How much would this cost without these details? Squinted at the Japanese. Pursed his lips at the estimate. Gave a couple of short nods.

I was surprised. There was never money for frills. Every winter we subsisted on unemployment funds since Dad worked outdoors—not possible in Canadian winters. And almost every year one of the three auto corporation workers went on strike, or the bus drivers did—meaning those populations had no money for new imitation brick siding on their homes—so Dad was on unemployment again. Every year Dad paid no more than one dollar for a Christmas tree—and now a landscaped front yard?

In a week it was all finished and very nice, uncluttered, easy to care for. Our house and yard no longer looked homemade, put together. The young man came once more to collect the balance due. He and Dad chatted amicably again. And it was done.

For years I wondered what made my father go ahead and spend such money on the landscaper's design. A real puzzle. The Japanese had not come on strong, no hard sell. A small discount. He was polite, respectful. I knew that in spring Dad had up to eight months of work to count on, money coming in. That wasn't really it though.

It took decades before it occurred to me. Japan and Germany were Axis powers, allies in the war. Dad would have known this—he must have kept himself well informed of the news during the war—how else to survive, escape the communists, even the SS in the last months? He'd always had a steadfast sense of respect for survival, hard work and competence. Something in the young Japanese spoke to him, and he responded.

Hey Nineteen!

After my sophomore year at the University of Windsor (no longer Assumption College), I had to cross the border to stay with my parents in Southfield, Michigan for the summer. We had immigrated to the United States from Canada the previous year, but I'd earned a scholarship and wanted to stay in Windsor where Marti lived. I knew no one in Michigan except two second cousins, whose most prominent features consisted of big bottle-bred black hair. I had to find a job. Not just to earn some money, but as much to get out of the house.

I tried for an office job, filing and whatnot—I couldn't really type. In one interview the guy told me I needed to wear more makeup. He should have hired one of my cousins. I ended up as a dayshift carhop at a Big Boy drive-in deep in Detroit.

One day during the lunchtime rush, I was carrying two trays out—one loaded with burgers, fries, cokes and shakes, the other had a Slim Jim and coffee. The latter was closer and simpler to negotiate, so I thought to get that out of the way, then deliver to the gang further on. I balanced the loaded tray with my left hand as I hooked the other onto a man's lowered window. He paid me, and as I was making change with my right hand, the tray in my left hand tipped, and its contents slid majestically through his window, onto his lap, all over his suit, his shirt, his tie—the works.

I stood in abject horror. He must have seen the terror on my face, because he said, "It's okay. Just go in and tell your manager what happened. They have insurance to cover this." I heard his words, but stayed frozen in disbelief and panic. I had an image of walking away, down the streets of Detroit to the Ambassador Bridge, back to Windsor… just away…never coming back.

But he said, "Don't worry," and repeated his instructions. I saw no way out, so I turned to do what he'd said. In my family, an event such as this was utterly disastrous—caustic with endless shame, blame and violence. That's what I dreaded as I entered the kitchen.

Stuttering, I told the manager, a pleasant, middle-aged woman. She didn't bat an eye, but dealt with the whole issue. I didn't even have to go out and see the poor man again. He was compensated for getting his suit cleaned, and I imagine he received a second Slim Jim. I don't remember who replaced the big order for the gang still waiting for their lunch.

What I do remember is the kindness and understanding of that man. And the matter-of- fact manner of the manager. I wasn't fired. No dirty looks, no scummy comments. No drama. A week or so later, The University of Windsor called to ask if I could come back to my library acquisitions job there for the rest of the summer.

Following the Trail to Meher Baba

The first time I saw Alfredo, Marti and I had just walked into Teutonia, the German Club, where we danced on Saturday nights. He was sitting with Tony, who, I later learned was his older brother, and a few other Italians. I was struck instantly by his face, and knew as we walked on to find an empty table that I would dance with no one but him. I had no way to explain this to Marti or to myself. Yes, he was very good-looking, which never hurts—blond wavy hair, clear blue eyes. But somehow I knew it was more than that—something in his face held me—but I couldn't know what for many years. Toward the end of the evening, I'd declined several offers to dance and the message got through to Alfredo. He came and asked me to dance. It was the last dance, so after we'd stood through "God Save the Queen," I started to talk. I found out that he spoke no English beyond yes, no, please, thank you. Just Italian.

I saw Alfredo a couple more times at Teutonia and we danced only with each other. Tony must have suggested we come to Caboto, the Italian Club, so Marti and I did, and found the music more lively than endless rounds of waltzes, foxtrots and polkas with an occasional boogie. Saturday nights then at Caboto with chachas, twists, sambas, along with foxtrots, and occasional waltzes and a rare polka. I danced only with Alfredo. We went for pizza afterward. Marti and I went to Caboto soccer games and practices. When my parents were out of town, I brought him home with me. I was totally in love.

At the same time I knew I would not marry him. I told him it was because he was Catholic and I was Lutheran, but I knew it wasn't just him being Catholic. I knew without knowing that my life needed to be bigger than a life with him. Perhaps as recompense I offered my virginity to him. It didn't matter. He wanted to marry. I was in my first year of university then and we began to see less of each other. One night I had a non-ordinary dream in which it was clear that it was over. It felt like my heart had been torn out. By the time I met Cliff in my senior year, I saw the announcement in the paper—Alfredo would marry a nurse. I have always hoped he'd have a happy life, a lovely and loving family.

The first time I saw Cliff was in a nightclub in Detroit in the fall of 1964. I went because my cousin, Renate, or Renee, as she called herself then, asked me to go there with her. It was an unusual request—we didn't see each other much any more. I was at loose ends after a summer of running around in Europe—Germany, Italy, France— and just starting my senior year at the University of Windsor. Cliff asked me to dance. He wasn't a good dancer (as Alfredo had been), so we shuffled around, which allowed me to silently sniff at this American's idea of dancing.

He was a Staff Sergeant in the Air Force, but not in uniform that evening. He'd spent time stationed near Frankfurt, Germany and enjoyed that very much. Also in North Africa, which he didn't much enjoy. He was interesting enough and wasn't bad looking (not nearly as handsome as Alfredo) and he seemed eager to please me. With no one else on the horizon and Marti seriously hooking up with Max, I accepted his offer to take me to see "Topkapi" with Melina Mercouri in Detroit next weekend. A date! He even picked me up in Windsor and brought me back. A couple of dates and then sex. Due to my family's history, I was utterly unwilling to be pregnant before marriage and utterly unwilling to have abortions, so I knew without thinking I had to marry Cliff. Mostly for the wrong reasons.

We married on March 6, 1965, a few months before I graduated. We moved into a two-room apartment in Windsor until I graduated, then rented a farm house north of Mount Clemens and near Selfridge Air Force Base. The day before I started birth control pills, I became pregnant with our first child, a lovely daughter, born in March 1966. Cliff and I were good at playing house, but we didn't know how to love each other. We each had unresolved hurts from our families and weren't able to keep from hurting each other. Our son was born almost three years later. In 1973 our divorce was final. He remarried almost immediately. I thought I would too, but that didn't happen. I went on a ten-year adventure which included sex, marijuana and travel. Trying to catch up on so-called good times.

The first time I saw Harry—actually I heard him first — laughing and laughing. His laughter rose up from the patio, wave after wave, flowing like Rapunzel's golden tresses up to my third floor room. It had a singular magic, unmooring unknown places deep within me. I was reading Kazantzakis' book, *The Last Temptation of Christ,* and the laughter leapt between the words, screwed the sentences until I gave up and put the book down. I went downstairs. I had to.

It was June 1973. I was at a three day Adult Education Conferene in Ypsilanti, Michigan, the first I'd been to since I started to teach English as a Second Language in Ferndale. As I walked out the door, I saw a small group sitting and standing in a loose circle on the patio. I stopped, waiting to see who was creating this laughter. It only took two seconds. I walked toward them, my eye on him. He saw me looking and he looked back at me. A Black man, tall, good-looking, about forty, slightly grey at the edges, a Boston Blackie moustache. A moment later I was offered a toke on a joint. I took it and I was in.

It didn't take long for the others to drift away, and I was alone with Harry. He asked me, "What do you go by?" I told him my name. "I don't do no Irma, Shep." I liked it—so cool. He taught English in the Detroit Adult Ed program. We didn't waste much time on chitchat—

whatever had gotten unmoored inside me was now chugging right along. We went up to my room in the dorm. I still remember our time there. What he said made me wild, what he did… almost calmed me down.

The next day at breakfast he told me he was married to a Filipino woman, had two kids with her, and two with his first wife—a quadroon—he made sure to tell me. An affair with a married man was not at the top of my list, but. I had to do it. Years later I heard a young woman come out of her counselor's office across the hall from mine, saying, "I've got my priorities." I knew what she meant.

We had our affair for a year. I wanted him all to myself of course, but I knew it didn't work that way. We talked marriage. He left his wife, moved in with a friend. One night I had him over for dinner, to meet my children. After they'd gone to bed, he criticized their table manners. That didn't feel right and I said something plain enough that the next time I talked to him, he said he was going back to his wife. I was in shock for two days. Cried. Couldn't go to work that evening. Couldn't sleep.

One year later we came together one more time. In 1981 I was back in Detroit for the summer, after my first trip to India. I called Harry to catch up, tell him about Meher Baba. I will always love him.

The first time I saw Donald Hill was in July 1975 on a bench in a park in the seaport of Pireus, Greece. How we got to that bench on that afternoon is another story, written elsewhere. We chatted, had dinner together and agreed to go to the beach the next day. He picked me up in downtown Athens in his VW camper and drove us to the beach. Over the rearview mirror was a small card with the photo of a young man with long dark hair standing in a thin white robe, his left hand holding his right wrist. When I asked who he was, Donald was vague—an Indian guru—no name.

When Donald showed up a year and a half later in Ferndale, Michigan, I began to sell my house and belongings. Donald showed me a passport photo of himself when he was younger—he looked just like Alfredo—same facial bone structure, same startling blue eyes, just his hair was dark rather than blonde. Somehow, I had been looking for this face. It wasn't until we were camping across the United States in my VW camper that I began very occasionally to hear the name—Meher Baba.

In the spring of 1980 in Venice Beach after Donald had died of emphysema and I had inherited that card, a poster of Baba and a book, *Listen, Humanity* that I began to want to believe that Meher Baba was who he said he was—God in human form. I deeply longed to believe that as I read *Listen, Humanity*. It was a short time later that one day, suddenly, without warning, I *knew* He was God in human form. This knowing has never left me. I had been blessed.

There are moments

when I feel I am
a hollow enough reed
to release a trace
of Your Love

I thought that first day would never end at the General Foods factory in Elmshorn, Germany. A whole long day of opening cardboard boxes and carrying them over to Deirdre from British Columbia, who stacked little boxes of cocoa powder into them, lifted the filled boxes onto a conveyer belt to whomever was next in line in this packing process. Hard to believe but I began to see the task of filling cardboard boxes as downright enjoyable. During the afternoon coffee break I asked Deirdre, tall, thin, freckled, if we could exchange places for a while, thinking that Deirdre too might appreciate a bit of change.

But no, she wouldn't change places. It stuck in my mind for decades to come that a woman with a name I'd never heard before was this rigid. The next day all thirteen of us had new jobs—packing boxes of rice into large cardboard boxes that came along on a conveyer belt. It was the first and the last time in my life that I fell asleep while standing on my feet.

We were all university students from across Canada. The West German government had invited 150 students who were studying German to fly Lufthansa from Montreal to Frankfurt, for a $100 round trip—an unbelievable deal even in 1964! The West German government wanted young Canadians to see the wall in Berlin. Brigitte, Jane, Art and I jumped at the chance, as did our German instructor, Father Weiler, at the University of Windsor.

When we landed in Frankfurt, we boarded one of three buses headed for Berlin. I was a bit hung over during the first part of the bus ride, from the two drinks I had on the flight. Lufthansa's drinking age rule differed from Ontario's, so at twenty, I ordered my first martini—found I couldn't handle another one of those, so ordered a Manhattan instead. And that was that— the first and last time for each of those concoctions for the rest of my life.

To break the monotony of the bus ride, some students started singing popular folksongs. Jane and I sang along. It was only later in life that the irony of singing "Hava Nagila" in Germany dawned on me. Many if not most of the students were either German-born or their parents were.

When we stopped in a town for lunch, we had to eat in relays because no restaurant could serve all of us at once. While I waited for my turn to order and eat, I stood in line for the WC. Two older German women came out of that door, one remarking to the other, *Wer sind die all hier?* Who are all these people? I understood immediately and thought I could respond more easily than some of my Canadian companions, whose first language had not been German. So I related to these women who we were and what we were doing there. The women listened and complimented me on my excellent command of the German language. I explained that I had, in fact, been born in Germany.

I didn't elaborate that though my parents claimed to be one hundred percent German, they had not been born or raised in Germany—my father in the Austro-Hungarian Empire and my mother in the same area, but it was Romania after WW I—both of German stock going back five generations, originally from the Pfalz area of the Rhine. I also left out that I'd been born in Krenau, twenty miles from Auschwitz—now Poland once more after the war.

As the two women listened to me, a critical gleam arose in their eyes. The one who had spoken even managed now to somehow look down her nose at me, despite being a foot shorter. *Well, if you were born in Germany, then your German should be much better!* I blinked and they walked away. I took a lesson from them and never bothered to relate my birthplace to a German again.

It began to dawn on me that Germans were not my favorite people. A quality I'd noted in German immigrants in Windsor—an intolerance of perceived imperfection came to mind. When I'd brought home my ninth grade class semester scores, my father demanded why I'd come second in algebra. "Because Henrietta's father is a professor of mathematics," I explained. My father accepted that— after all, though he was good at doing math in his head, he had no idea what algebra was.

It wasn't exactly that I had 'favorite people.' The first friend I'd ever had in my life was a Black girl. The next was Scottish-Polish. Several neighborhood friends were

French Canadian. My current best friend since high school was Latvian. And here was Deirdre from British Columbia, who never became a friend.

We had two days in Berlin, staying in a youth hostel — bunk beds and ample breakfasts. Saw the Wall and toured the museums set up in the neighboring houses, whose narrow flights of stairs set off impressions of real flight across night time rooftops. Listened to stories of successful escapes over the wall from East Berlin and un-successful ones too. Jane and I went through Checkpoint Charlie to see East Berlin—half buried still in piles of rubble and store windows sparsely decorated with half a dozen items—hohum to the Western eye.

The West Germans' organization was remarkable. For those of us willing, we were assigned jobs and families to live with. Jane and I settled in a village near the Danish border with the Scheelkes, whose nineteen-year-old son, Karl-Heinz, worked in the General Foods offices in Elmshorn.

Every week or so the General Foods forewoman called out *Sauber machen!* Cleanup time! That meant all thirteen of us were sweeping, dusting, scouring, picking up de-bris until the current work area was sparkling before we moved on to the next packing project. This was such a welcome shift that my mind and body relished these simple but varied tasks.

One day I was asked to begin a new job, packing instant coffee into tiny single-serving tubes. I figured I was chosen because I was the only native speaker of German among the thirteen Canadian students there. In a separate room I was trained to fill spaces in a machine with the empty metal tubes, which were open at one end. When the machine was turned on, it rotated to fill each tube with instant powdered coffee and seal it. Then I was to remove the filled tubes and put them into a cardboard box. Over and over. Again and again. That would have become boring in itself, but the truly horrendous part was being right next to the machine, which emanated a bone-crushing, ear-splitting cacophony as it performed its mechanical task. I despaired of getting through the day without permanent hearing loss if not incipient brain wave damage.

Suddenly the forewoman came to tell me that there was a phone call for me. What!? Having no idea who could be calling me, I left the machine and went to the phone in another room. It was Marga! I had boarded with Marga's aunt and her family for the first two years of university. She had left Windsor to return to Germany to help look after her own mother. How wonderful to hear from her here and now! I had written to Marga after I'd settled in with the German/Danish family I boarded with. How did she find me here? We chatted for a bit. I didn't get to see Marga ever again to tell her how her phone call had somehow saved me from ever again having to abide the raucous screeching of the coffee packing machine.

I stuck with the rest of the packing tasks—rounds of cocoa and for the next few weeks, saving the few Marks that were left over after paying for my room and board with the German/Danish family. After six weeks of this, mid-July, Marti flew in from Windsor, slept on a cot in our attic loft for a few nights. It didn't make sense to keep on packing at General Foods now. I cabled my parents, asking for $300 to travel with. They sent it. And off we went—Jane to relatives in Zagreb, Yugoslavia, while Marti and I traipsed through Germany, Italy and France for the rest of the summer.

Crash! A Lesson

In the summer of 1965 I had graduated from the University of Windsor and newly married, I moved with my American husband to Michigan, to a farmhouse he'd rented near the Air Force Base where he was stationed. One day I drove back across the Detroit-Windsor Tunnel, to spend a last day with Marti. She and her new husband were about to fly to Ghana, to serve two years in the Canadian version of the Peace Corps. We had a lovely, carefree day—no looming papers to write, no exams to study for—and then I headed back to the Tunnel. On the way I stopped at a liquor store and bought a bottle of Hiram Walker's Canadian Club whiskey, made in Windsor—I knew my husband would enjoy this.

I was practiced at smuggling things across the border — clothes, cats and now alcohol. After an hour's drive, I pulled onto our driveway, stopped the car and gathered all my stuff to take inside, including the bottle of Canadian Club. Hanging on to purse, shopping bag, sweater and whiskey, I climbed out of the car and began to walk toward the kitchen door. I'd barely gone three steps when I felt something slip from under my arm and *CRASH* onto the concrete sidewalk. No-o-o! The Canadian Club! Glass all over the sidewalk. Liquor seeping into the grass. No-o-o! I stood in shock. Looked up into the skyblue sky and said, "Yes. Okay...I get it..." as if God was really up there. "...no more smuggling."

Your frown shakes me down,

but You say,
"Thank Me for your difficulties—
through suffering you can open
to My Love."

Your belighted smile keeps me alive
To Your Love.

When It's My Time

The first time I saw a person's dead body was in 1968, when I was pregnant with my second child. My mother-in-law's Scottish-Canadian father had died. Cliff and I went to the funeral home in Royal Oak, Michigan. I'd met her father two or three times during holidays, but never had a conversation with him, so whatever I knew about him had come from Catherine. As I stepped up to the casket and looked at his body, I burst into convulsive tears. I lost control of myself. The tears didn't stop until some time after I'd left the room. I had no idea what caused me to weep like that. I hardly knew the man.

Decades later, it occurred to me that upon seeing a dead body for the first time, while I was pregnant with Alex, that I'd had an unconscious premonition of his early death. It was the only explanation that made any sense to me. I never saw Alex's body after his car crash on September 18, 1987, when he was eighteen, but he came to me through an extraordinary 'dream' two days later. I saw him as he might have looked after he'd been thrown from his car—bones sticking out, bloody scrapes—but he appeared triumphant—his face shining at me. As if to say, "It's okay, Mom. It had to happen. I did good." As a little guy, one of Alex's favorite games was to play "smash 'em up" with his matchbox cars. I tell myself the story that he'd been responsible for someone's death in a car crash in a past life, and that his crash and death now balanced his karma so he could move forward.

When my mother died by taking a handful of whatever she kept stashed away for those times when despair overwhelmed her, she was in her Ford Galaxy in their garage. The motor had stopped running, but the radio still blared. Her doctor had taken her off all medications a few weeks earlier to rest her kidneys. So this handful of pills did what she'd been threatening to do for decades.

The police called me at 6 A.M. on Sunday morning, October 3, 1971, telling me to come to my parents' house as soon as possible. They wouldn't tell me why. But I knew. "She's finally done it," I said to Cliff. Her body was still in the car in the open garage when I pulled up. Police in the driveway behind the house. I stepped out, glanced at the garage, saw my father standing on the back porch, looking lost. *Look to the living*, came to me in that instant. So I climbed the porch steps and embraced my father.

When Ilse, came from Opa-Locka, Florida the next day, she wanted to see Mom's body. There was to be no funeral or showing, but the funeral home allowed her and Dad to view Mom's body. Unwilling to see what she had done to herself, I chose not to. I stayed in the waiting room. "You'll be sorry when I'm gone," Mom had said to me repeatedly. I never was. I was relieved.

Donald's body was next, on March 20, 1980 in Venice Beach. I was the first to see him and lift him off the oxygen machine after he'd died. Pagan, nine, wouldn't look at him. I learned later that the first person to touch a dead body takes on at least some of the dead person's *sanskaras*. Some weeks after he'd died, I was leaving my studio apartment one day and saw a lone dog in the alley, about fifteen feet from me. We stood staring at each other for a long moment. Suddenly he yelped, jumped straight up in a panicked twist—landed and scuttled off as fast as he could. Puzzled, I stared after him. No idea what had happened. Later I learned that Parsis, Iranian Zoroastrians, bring a dog to the body of someone who has just died, to take on the dead person's *sanskaras.* Perhaps that that dog took Donald's *sanskaras* from me.

My father died of kidney failure in January 1990 in Beaumont Hospital (the same hospital where Alex had been born), in Royal Oak, Michigan. I saw him every day for a week, ten days before he died. He didn't look like the father I had known. I held his hand as convulsions swept through his body. I said Meher Baba's prayers at his bedside. After Luella called me in Tucson to say he had passed, I wept and keened for hours. I didn't understand why. He was eighty-six and at peace with dying. I was at peace with his dying too. So why the keening? The wailing? I had never done that before. Perhaps it was now safe to let unresolved grief from the past come up and out now. There was no funeral. I didn't see his body. I did visit his gravesite in Royal Oak with Luella a year later.

In 1994 Karl and I went to see his Aunt Kathleen's body a day or two after she'd died, though she had said she didn't want us to see her that way. I saw a lifeless, waxen form—the-who-she-was, wasn't there. I was uncomfortably aware that her subtle body might be hovering and I felt nervous, knowing that she hadn't wanted us to see her corpse. We said our prayers and left.

Our beloved little black cat, Sushi, died early in March 1997. She'd been ill and wasn't eating. Multiple visits to two vets ended with our decision to not torment her with further treatments. To let her go. We buried her under a eucalyptus tree in our back yard, wrapped in a scarf Stephanie had brought from India and in a tiny afghan Luella had knitted especially for Sushi. We said prayers and we wept. Sushi was the most nearly perfect cat. We adored her. She owned us. Next life, we'd told her, she'd move on to be a dawg. I wept for three days, missing our delightful little cat.

My sister also died in Florida in March 1997, of complications from rheumatoid arthritis—her intestines leaked and couldn't be repaired. After some days, her children agreed to disconnect the lifelines and let their mother go. Ilse and I had not been in communication for the previous six years— misunderstandings and unresolved emotions. Either just before or just after she died, she came to me in a non-ordinary dream—we had significant eye contact—a connection again. Some kind of agreement—my best guess was that she wanted me to stay in touch with her children and I agreed. No tears.

Her middle child, Kurt, died of cancer about fourteen years later. Her eldest, my godson, Kim shot himself, in total despair of getting his rig to run right so he could work. Money, work, women, alcohol, a gun. Five years earlier we'd met for lunch at the Triple T Truck Stop in Tucson. I hadn't seen him in twenty-five years, but we'd talked regularly on the phone. He proudly showed me his new rig.

"I'm your godmother," I told him, "so I'm supposed to tell you about God. This is Meher Baba (I showed him a card with Baba's picture), He says He is God. Would you put His picture up on the sun visor of your rig?" "Sure," he said, and put it up, assuring me on the phone over the next years that he still had Meher Baba watching over him in his rig. When he traded that rig in for a newer one, he assured me again that he'd put Baba's picture up.

His sister, Lori, had Kim's body cremated. Karl and I rendezvoused with her in Waycross, Georgia in October 2018. At my sister's former home, ashes of Lori's mother, Ilse, her father, Gren and my mother, Eleonore, were buried. We added the ashes of Kim, Lori's husband, Sean, and ashes of photos of my father, Edmund and nephew, Kurt. Said Meher Baba's prayers, sang "Amazing Grace" and "Welcome To My World." Lori asked to keep her copy of the prayers. I offered a Baba button and she was glad to have it—tells me she has the Baba button up in her van—Baba is watching over her. She's reading stories of how people came to Baba. We talk often. She plans to visit us again this summer with her new dog, Baloo.

Karl's father, Walt, died of lung cancer in our Tucson duplex in April 2001. His hospice caregiver knocked on my door that morning, saying Walt had died in the night and I should come to confirm what she said. I followed her next door and saw he'd fallen off his bed, his body stiff in the position of his fall. I called Karl at work and he called the funeral home where Walt's body would be cremated. The caregiver stayed to clean Walt's body and I left her to it. When two young men came for his body, I went to observe and help in any way I could. Watched them put the corpse, still bent up in rigor mortis, on a sheet and with each man holding two corners of the sheet, they carried Walt's naked body out the kitchen door. I'm sure Walt would not have wanted me to see this. I was relieved that Karl didn't see this. I never described it to him.

I'm pretty sure Cliff is dead now, perhaps since 2013 or 2014. His last FaceBook entry in 2013 showed him in the Philippines in a wheelchair, with oxygen and a sign that said "emphysema." I wouldn't have recognized him—gaunt, teeth missing, his thick dark hair mostly gone. A note said, "I wish I'd stopped smoking sooner." Like Donald, minus the cool.

Minnie and Max, brother and sister cats were seventeen years old when they passed. A bobcat climbed the fir tree in front of our house, jumped on the roof and down into the back yard. Found Max and was faster than him…I chased the bobcat off, found Max under the Texas Ranger hedge. We buried him with prayers and tears in a corner of the cat yard. Three weeks later, Minnie, already blind, stopped eating, was walking in slow tight circles. We called someone in and let Minnie go as she lay on my lap. We buried her next to Max with prayers and tears—our furry companions for the past seventeen years.

We assume that ZemZem, another little black cat has gone too. Somehow she'd found a way out of our well-fortified back yard—twice in August 2015 I'd found her in the front driveway stalking a bird early in the mornings. On the third day, she was gone. Very possibly a coyote got her. It would have been quick.

Norm Darwish died in Michigan. It was through him that Karl and I met in Detroit. Nancy Wall, my writing godmother, died of pancreatic cancer in April 2018 in Tucson. Baba lover Lewis Stickford died of cancer in 2019. He and Stephen Shev, who died several years ago of heart failure, had been born in the same year as I.

So many different kinds of deaths. They're all gone now. So many losses. After each one, my heart settles into an altered rhythm. In this life, how will I go when it's my time?

Dream by the Sea

I come to the shore, sea fringes lacy with salt,
the surface calm.
He stands there alone, tall and straight,
awaiting me.

I walk just past him, step into the sea's fringe,
let the foamy water cool my feet.
We are much alike, he says to me, quiet and clear.
I turn to look at this man.

He has just said words I now recognize
I have so longed to hear.
My heart is glad.
I awake to the five o'clock morning.

However long
I need the scaffolding
of this body to swivel in this chair—
it is my heart
that He is building
strong and true.

Bosses

In 1973 I took a job teaching English as a Second Language in the Adult Education program at our local high school in Ferndale, Michigan. Before classes began, all the Adult Ed teachers met with our supervisor, Anna Mae Burdi, in one of the classrooms. I had always kept a circumspect distance from bosses—I did my job well and was respectful, but never close or chummy—due to my experiences with my mother and my older sister, who entertained no question of whether they were my bosses.

My mother's essential message was: *Do what I say, or else.* This meant violence or abandonment could ensue. My sister's version was: *Do what I say, don't do what I do.* The threat there promised exclusion. I trusted neither.

Anna Mae—first name basis right off—spoke in front of the classroom, outlining the program, which highlighted the motto, "You Can!" She listed the goals and expectations. She ended with this: *Your job is to teach English, math, history or civics. My job is to help you do your job.*

I had never heard anyone who had authority over me verbally put herself at my service. It set the standard forever. I knew then what a supervisor's job truly entailed. With her dictum, Mom got lots of barebones work out of me. My sister's mixed message at times led me astray. The deep truth of Anna Mae's commitment penetrated my psyche, and I put my heart into teaching.

joyful otter

under flat-footed clouds I slide carefree
between ocean drops
furred feet beating praise
I thread through kelp and weed.
Wetness christens my soul --
I glide and soar, dive
flipflip and roar at wily seahorses.
Lissom, limber
beyond dreams I zing
the unstruck music with salty delight,
float on a seaswell,
crack open mussels and
clams on my belly ,
play tag, touch, chase ruck and tuck
fast with my fellows.
Squeak surrender, show teeth
to the elusive green sunset ray.
I know only this wide ecstatic sea,
this drunken sun that winks
and falls for me,
this ravishing joy

On the Bench

The first time I saw Donald Hill I was sitting on a park bench in Piraeus, Greece, on a Saturday afternoon, early in July 1975. I was resting from a day of shopping and sightseeing in Athens and Piraeus. When I first walked into the park, I saw only clusters of men. Remembering that Melina Mercouri played a big-hearted prostitute in Piraeus in the movie, "Never On Sunday," I backed out, walked around the park's edge till I saw an area with women and children, found an empty bench and sat. First I wrote in my new notebook—details of how I came to be there just then, and an honest analysis of the men in my life at the time, recognizing there was not one I could seriously consider trying to make a life with. Then I opened my new *Time* magazine and began to read it.

After a few minutes, a quick glance suggested that an old Greek man had seated himself at the other end of the bench. I ignored him too. Until suddenly he said, "Is that the latest *Time* magazine?" He was not Greek, but American. This was Donald. We began to chat.

Donald, the black sheep of a Boston banking family, in jeans and a denim shirt, carrying a daypack. Startling blue eyes. Grey hair. Deep voice. Facial features strongly resembling my father. Wiry build, like my father too, but two or three inches shorter than me. For once I just didn't care about that—something reassuring in his oh so cool manner. He had just seen friends off on their way to

Crete. He was to follow them on Monday. My story was that I'd somehow been bumped off a flight to Samos, and would fly there on Monday. I don't remember what all we told each other there on the bench. I do remember telling him something I'd never told anyone before.

I was fifteen, trying to fall sleep one night in November 1958, when suddenly I was in a different state of consciousness. I had no awareness of my body—only of *knowing* that I was not this body, this identity of Irma — that whatever I was, was something utterly, blissfully beyond that. I didn't know how long I was in that state. When I returned to normal consciousness, all I wanted to do was to go back. But I didn't know how. I had no language to describe this and no one to tell it to.

Donald seemed to know what I was talking about.

As dusk fell, he said, "I'm getting hungry—do you want to find some dinner with me?" Yes. We did that. Since we were both at loose ends, he invited me to go to the beach with him the next day. He picked me up in downtown Athens and we had a sunny day at the beach. In his VW camper, I saw a card fastened above the rearview mirror —a picture of a young man with long dark, hair, standing with one hand clasped on his arm. "Who is that?" He gave me a vague answer—an Indian guru.

Donald told me he, his wife, Kathy and their four-year-old daughter, Pagan, had been camping from Amsterdam through Europe to Morocco, on their way to India. But in Marrakesh they'd had a falling out, and she and Pagan returned to the United States. Now he was on his way to India by himself. It all sounded so exotic to me.

We agreed to meet up after our respective visits to Crete and Samos and camp around Greece together. The focus of my summer, of my whole life, had just shifted in ways of which I had no clue. A week later, there was a moment on a rooftop garden on Samos, in the shade of a lemon tree, when I thought I could die now and be satisfied with the life I'd had so far.

Little did I know!

Letting Go

Letting go of what I know—
stepping into the Now.

Leaving Germany, 1948

Showing off my watch, Goyeau
Street, Windsor, 1949

Rear: Richie, Aunt Pauline, June, Uncle Dick
Front: Irma and Ilse. Long Island, 1951

Mother's Day photo, Ilse and Irma

Brigitte, Irma, Art, Lufthansa 1964

Irma and Jane, packing cocoa, Elmshorn Germany 1964

With Marti in Paris, 1964

B.A. graduation 1965

Cliff, Irma, Stephanie 1966

Anna Mae Burdi 1973

Irma and Ilse, 1981

Donald in Greece 1975

My VW camper
Los Angeles 1978

Donald, Richard and Pagan Hill
Venice Beach 1979

Mimi's treat for Stephanie's 12th birthday, Venice Beach 1978

With Donald and Pagan, Long Beach, CA 1980

Filis Frederick

Irma leaving Venice Beach 1980

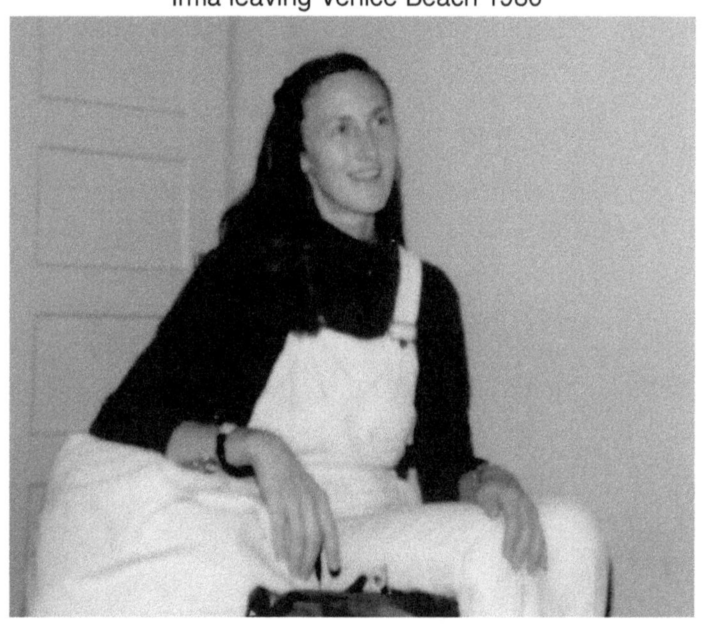

Dad and Luella, Michigan

Martha and Matthew, Michigan 1981

In Norfolk, VA 1982

Alex, Pagan, and Felix, Norfolk, VA 1982

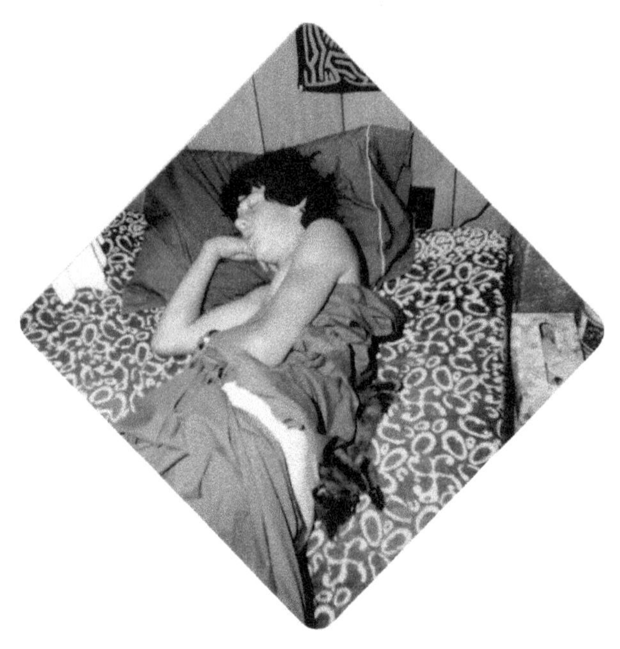

Alex in Virginia Beach, 1982

Sailing with Alex, Norfolk1982

Karl and Irma, aka 'Karma,' just married, Tucson 1983

Karl, Alex and Robert, Pima Canyon, Christmas 1986

Karl, Alex play racquetball, Christmas 1986

With Alex after pizza, Detroit

Stephanie's graduation, Michigan 1987

...at Luella's, Royal Oak, Michigan 1987

...at Luella's, Royal Oak, Michigan 1987

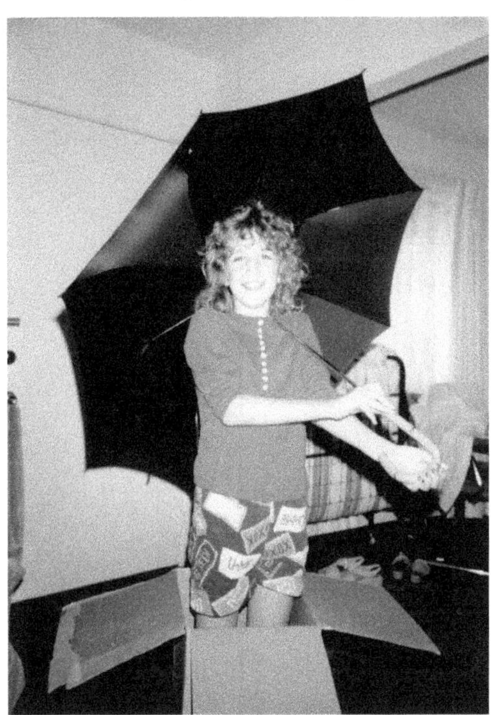

Danielle

ALEXANDER LEE SHEPPARD
JAN. 15, 1969
SEPT. 18, 1987
HE TOUCHED MANY LIVES

Prayer

EDMUND HEXEL
1904 - 1990

With Stephanie in Tucson 1988

Gifts of Age writing group
Nancy Wall, rear, second from right
Irma, front center

With Kathy Hill, Myrtle Beach SC

Karl and father Walt in Tucson 2000

Ben, Ru, and Ching-Fen, Tucson 2011

In Sakori, India 2010

Charles Haynes, Myrtle Beach

Jeff Wolverton, Myrtle Beach

Last days in
Tucson

Sasha guarding
the back deck,
Asheville NC

SKYLIFT PARK
GATLINBURG
19 September 2019
Great Smoky Mountains

Karma

Watching and Waiting

The first time I saw Meher Baba's picture was in Piraeus, Greece. Donald had it on a card taped above the rearview mirror of his VW camper. Baba, young and looking like Jesus, standing with one hand holding the wrist of the other. I asked Donald, *Who is that?* An Indian guru, he said. I wasn't interested enough to pursue it, but I never forgot I saw Him there. He saw us too, as we camped around the Peloponnesian Peninsula the summer of 1975, smoking hash Donald had been given in Marrakesh, telling each other stories—of adventure and travels, books and authors we enjoyed, loves found and lost, funny and sad, making love…it was all so exotic. I wanted more!

All this with Baba, silent, watching and listening from His perch above the rearview mirror—looking back at us. And me looking forward to each day, each town with its beach, its *plaka* and homey restaurants, where we peeked into their kitchen pots to see what looked good that day. Playing Scrabble on the beach, sun warming our fingers, our hearts, getting us ready for the evening—the smoke, the sex…And Baba, young, standing with His hand and wrist joined, watching and waiting for the day, the year, the moment, when He knew I would be ready, finally ready, to hear His call, His word, His song and *know* Who He *really* is.

While I Was Waiting

While I was waiting for Donald to show up in Ferndale, he was hanging out with his sister, he wrote, in the outskirts of Paris. When he arrived over a year later, he talked about a woman in Paris whose breast implants leaked and imploded. I thought her silly to get such things under her skin—it barely occurred to me that he'd been doing her. I could hardly complain, though, because I'd hooked up with Herb, an ex-biker, retired from that life already at the age of 32—same age as me. I met Herb in a bar, where Marty and I went to dance early in 1976.

Waiting for Donald and desperate for some kind of support as a single mom, I invited Herb to live with my kids and me. He didn't turn out to be much of a support though—worked as spaghetti cook for a while, and after he left the restaurant, he cooked for us. A lot of crazy, scary stuff was going on then—smoking dope, parties—I got it that I was a bit out of control. Years later I wondered what I'd been doing with this man!

Years later, after I'd told Herb he had to go, after I left Ferndale with Donald and my daughter to camp across the country for five months, after I lived in Venice Beach for three years, after Donald died of emphysema, after God in the form of Meher Baba made Himself known to me, after I had some perspective of all that earlier desperation—then one day I was going through my photographs and saw one of Herb showing my son how to do something, and there was something oddly familiar in Herb's profile. It didn't register right away…took time before it hit me—*really*?!

There was a definite hint of resemblance between Herb's profile and that of Meher Baba. How was that possible? Herb had lost his teeth in barroom brawls and got a set of false teeth, which he rarely wore. This caused me to determine I would do my best never to have false teeth. But Baba too, lost almost all of His teeth while descending from the Beyond Beyond state back into the gross plane of consciousness, which was so utterly intense that He would bang His forehead on a stone in His room in Poona, India. Then wear a turban to cover the bloody wound so His mother wouldn't get upset. Over and over…and banged His teeth loose. Later, Eruch talked Him into getting a set of false teeth, but He rarely wore them. So Baba and Herb did indeed have an aspect of similarity in their profiles. Some part of me had recognized this and was attracted to it, long before I ever heard Meher Baba's name. Some people might call this a breadcrumb on the path of finding Him.

Winner's Circle

no candy cotton prize pulls me to the wire
it's a lapis true heart pumping
for the pearl

Whoever There Is, Help Me

In May 1977, at the end of the spring semester, our outreach ESL classes in Ferndale had a farewell potluck lunch. For me, it really was a farewell, because I'd sold my house and either sold or given away almost all of my possessions. My son had gone to live with his father. My daughter, my friend, Donald and I were set up to camp across the country in my VW poptop camper. Leaving my life in Michigan.

Students invited their family members to the potluck. One of the students in my beginning ESL class was a middle-aged Iranian woman, who was quiet and very shy. I had gently encouraged her to begin to speak English words and phrases, praised her steps forward and was pleased at the progress she made. She brought a giant rice pilaf to the potluck and her husband, who was a retired general from Shah Pahlavi's Iranian army.

He thanked me profusely for the helpful encouragement I'd given his wife to begin speaking English—apparently it had been quite a challenge for her. In his enthusiasm, he said to me, "If you ever need anything, just call me."

Aside from the fact that I didn't have any of his contact information, and aside from the fact that I never felt the need to call on him, and aside from the fact that two years later, the Shah was deposed and he fled Iran—so presumably any power the general had had, had now evaporated—in spite of all these things, I never forgot what he had said to me.

Midsummer 1978, I took a job as recreation director at Hirschhorn Board & Care Home in Santa Monica, California. It paid minimum wage plus two meals each working day, and it gave me a lot of freedom to schedule events in the OT shop and trips to places and events all over Los Angeles County.

Sometime in 1979, Donald was diagnosed with emphysema and he was not doing well at all. I had gladly given up my life in Michigan, and sadly given up my children one by one to live with their father in Illinois. My own health was waning at the age of thirty-six, due to smoking non-filtered Camels and dope—and now I felt the walls of illusion had become increasingly slippery. I had counted on Donald for direction—now he was gasping on his bed. In my growing sense of helplessness, I needed something to hang onto. I strung some colored wooden beads together, with the idea of using this to count prayers, but I ended up just holding the beaded strand as I fell asleep. Needing something to hang on to.

Donald had told me a little bit about Meher Baba. Once he related something Meher Baba had said. I said, "Who does he think he is, God?" And Donald said, "He says he is." I said nothing, but thought, "This one says he's God and that one says he's God. You're God, I'm God—everybody's God."

One evening, after I'd finished work, I locked the OT shop door and spread a mat on the cement floor. Desperate to reach out to Something greater than myself, I sat on the mat with my coloreds beads and began to chant, *Om nam renge kyo.* After barely a minute of chanting, I was aware that it had no meaning for me. I read later that this chant is a pledge to oneself to never yield to difficulties and to win over one's suffering.

I sat in the gentle dark for some moments and gathered myself to say, *Whatever, Whoever there Is, help me. Please help me.*

Donald, his two children living with us by then and I managed somehow to keep on keeping on for the next several months. Then Donald died on the first day of spring, March 20, 1980. I inherited his two pictures of Meher Baba and a book by and about him, *Listen, Humanity.* In my grief I read this book and found that I wanted to believe that Meher Baba was who he said he was— God in human form.

One day in May 1980, I had the sudden unexpected experience of *knowing* that Baba was Who He said He was— *Meher Baba was God!* At first I thought I'd gone cuckoo, but the *knowing* never want away. Never. I was inexplicably joyous for a few weeks. On Friday, June 13, I went to my first Meher Baba meeting in Los Angeles.

Meher Baba was born Merwan Sheriar Irani. His father was from Iran and his mother was from a Parsi family in Poona, India. Decades later, I wondered if the Iranian general's offer had actually been Meher Baba's words to me—Baba speaking through him. I had sat humbly on the mat on the floor and asked for help. The knowing that Meher Baba is God came to me at a time I was emptying mind and heart—making room for what was Real.

Do your best. Leave the results to me. I have already taken care of everything. Don't worry, be happy in My Love.

Once in 1994, Baba said to me, *Just do what's in front of you. I will put everything you need right in front of you.* This message has given me the courage and strength to step into the unknown several times since then.

I began to connect the Iranian general's offer of help, my asking God for help and God making Himself known within me—the beaded strand I'd made in Venice had transformed into *a garland of life-giving Love.*

I called You

and You came.
I called You
though I didn't
know Your Name.
I called You
and You came.

Every time

I think perhaps I'm done with this life's deeds,
ready, perhaps, to leave this form,
I see suddenly a window
where there was none before,
and then a door,
which I'm suddenly through
and into the next vast adventure—
yet still
still in Your arms

"Can you help me?"

Donald's question rooted me into that long moment. I got it at once that our relationship had just taken another radical turn. I was crouched at the foot of his mattress on the floor, looking into his still clear blue eyes—direct and plainly asking—requiring me to shift immediately into an 'in charge' place within myself. An edgy vibration passed through me. His question seemed to hang in the air between us as he sat on his mattress, leaning forward, wheezing. Of course I wanted to help him. But how?

Donald's health had been deteriorating for weeks, if not months. We were home alone at this moment—his eight-year-old daughter, Pagan, was at school and his twenty-six-year-old son, Richard, was out somewhere, probably in my VW camper. A few months earlier, due to his declining health, Donald had asked me to sleep in the other room, with Richard, on opposite walls so Donald could have the bed to himself, with a bed for Pagan in a corner. A hippie lifestyle.

His question reverberated in my mind. "Yes. What can I do to help you?"

"Can you get a doctor to come and see me here?"

The logistics of that idea flew instantly beyond the realm of unlikelyhood and into the realm of the undoable. It wouldn't work. The reasons shot through my brain like a scatter of crows. Neither Donald nor I knew any doctor in Los Angeles. He had no health insurance. He had very little money. I had no clue about social services in L.A. Still, for two seconds I imagined myself calling a doctor and explaining to a receptionist what Donald wanted. Even in my imagination, I couldn't fathom being convincing enough to get a doctor to come to our two-room apartment in Venice Beach. I knew I didn't have the brass to even try. How to tell this to Donald and not lose face?

"I could take you to the Emergency at a hospital." Even that felt iffy. The only hospital I knew of was in Playa Del Rey, where I'd take my eleven-year-old daughter when she'd broken her arm a year earlier.

"No...no."

"At the Emergency you could tell them you're a vet from WW II." When we'd met in Piraeus, Greece four years earlier, and camped all summer around the Peloponnesian peninsula, he'd told me stories of his U.S. Army stint in India—how his company got all shot up and he almost the sole survivor was put in charge of a troop of Gurkhas, who crawled on their bellies with knives in their teeth... (Decades later, Pagan's mother sent me a copy of Donald's journal, which told a very different story...maybe he'd been dishonorably discharged?).

"No—try to get a doctor to come and see me here."

I was floundering. His asthma was much worse—coughing and wheezing—ugly stuff. Yet he was still smoking Camels and dope. I knew he was truly ill, but I didn't see that a doctor would make a house call in 1979. Maybe if he'd been a Kennedy—he'd told me he used to play touch football with those boys as a kid. As much as I wanted to please Donald, to have him think well of me, as he once had—I just did not see this happening.

We heard the kitchen door open. Richard came in. Without forethought, I stood and faced him. "I'm glad you're home, Richard. Donald is very ill, He needs to go to the hospital. Will you take him to the Emergency now?"
"Uh, yeah. Sure."

What else could he have said? Good. I was off the hook. It was more appropriate for a relative to take Donald in anyway. More of a son's job than a housemate's—that's what our relationship had devolved into.

As Donald and Richard got ready to go to the Emergency, I got ready to go to work in Santa Monica. I'd take the bus, as I often did, leaving the VW camper for them to use if they needed it. I felt great relief now that the pressure was off. As I waited for the bus, I thought about how Donald might be pissed at me—he had set aside his pride in asking me for help, but likely felt it much diminished in needing his son to help him. I still felt it to be the most appropriate recourse. I had, in fact, helped him to get the help he needed.

This Fountain of Oneness

There is only one dying—
to leave off what I want.

How to live then?

Give Me everything, He says,
and I will give you Nothing.

Ozone Walkway

Among the three of us we had no idea of what to do about Donald's hacking cough. His life long asthma was getting worse and it was harder for him to breathe. But he still smoked Camels unfiltered and dope when any one of us scored. Not Pagan, of course—she was only nine—sunny and a good sport about everything—never pouting or whining. Donald's son, Richard was twenty-six and he had sources though he was new to California. The four of us lived in a two-room apartment with a galley kitchen on Ozone Walkway in Venice Beach. Half a block from the Pacific.

I had no idea either until the morning Donald and I were home alone and he asked me if I could help him. Of course I wanted to help him, but what he wanted was beyond anything I felt capable of—no doctor would come to see him here. Richard took Donald to Emergency, got a doctor and a diagnosis of emphysema — lungs turning to leather—meds and a breathing machine. An order to quit smoking.

That was in the summer of 1979. By the end of summer Richard decided to go back to Boston. Then we were three in the two-room place. I took Donald to the Emergency around 3 or 4 A.M. a couple of times, then mid-November he had to stay in the hospital for several days. I took Pagan to work with me after her school day was done. I worked as the recreation director at Hirschhor-Board and Care on Pico Blvd. in Santa Monica from 11 A.M. to 8 P.M. Tuesday through Saturday. It was easy to include Pagan in any activities—she was easy to be around. On Thanksgiving Day she helped me and a few residents make pumpkin pies for everyone, and then I took her to the hospital to see Donald.

We got to the door of his room and heard an explosive eruption coming from a racked up human form. A nurse already there. We turned heel and hustled back down the corridor, Pagan gasping, "That was not Donald! *That was not Donald!!*" It was him. It was. But I didn't say anything. We scooted off, got ice cream on the Venice Board-walk, sat on a bench. Watched the gulls and the Pacific waves roll in and the rollerskaters whiz by... Walked slowly to our Ozone apartment.

At the hospital they cleaned out Donald's lungs big time, so when I brought him home days later he could breathe pretty well, and he could walk and drive—almost nor-mal. That was the upside. The downside, at least for me, was that he spent almost all his time with Pagan when she was home from school. Doing her homework, play-ing games. Well yes, of course. I'd be lying on my bed, reading, hearing them chat and chuckle, envious, jealous even—not good for me. I needed silence and space from them. I needed to get away. Donald was well enough now to look after himself and Pagan too.

I found a sweet second floor studio apartment just a few blocks away on Paloma Walkway. Nice wood floor, built in bed, kitchenette. A view of the Pacific from my bathroom window. I left my VW camper in the parking lot behind the Ozone apartment, so Donald could use it as needed. I took a bus to work. I had use of a van there for recreational outings with the residents and could easily make an extra stop for my own needs. I ate lunch and dinner in the Hirschhorn dining room, so I hardly needed much at my own place. I moved in before Christmas.

Looking back at the summer with four of us squashed into two rooms, sleeping on foam on the floor—none of us knowing how it would all come out—in just a few weeks, a month or two and all our lives had changed.

Knowing comes only
by God's Grace—all I can do
is empty my self.

"Are You Okay for the Night?"

The last time I saw Donald alive was about eight in the evening of March 20, 1980 in his apartment at 45 Ozone Walkway in Venice Beach. I had made dinner for Donald, Pagan and myself. After I'd cleaned up I felt the need for both a cigarette in the privacy of my own studio apartment a few blocks away, and a good night's sleep in my own bed. He had asked me a few weeks earlier if I would sleep in their apartment once again—he didn't want Pagan to wake up one morning to find his dead body. I had agreed, but didn't sleep well there—too many difficult memories.

When I had moved into the two-room place with him, Pagan and Richard in the fall of 1978, I felt like an outsider to this family. Donald was increasingly distant with me, though Pagan was always sweet with me, and Richard unfailingly considerate. When Donald developed emphysema a year later, his coolness increased, and I sensed it wasn't just about his illness. It wasn't until decades later, when Kathy, Pagan's mother, sent me a copy of Donald's journal to read, asking me to then send it on to Pagan, that I understood—he'd meant to leave me for another woman. When that didn't work out (she didn't like Pagan being around), I was his only other option. Not knowing any of this, I still felt deeply the pain of the loss of affection and regard between us.

After Richard returned to Boston late in 1979, I soon couldn't bear to overhear the sweet and intimate conversations between Donald and Pagan. They underlined my own sense of being alone, on the outside. It was such a contrast to the honeymoon intimacy he and I had had camping in Greece a few years earlier. I looked for and found a sweet studio apartment nearby. He seemed to be relieved that I was moving out.

So after dinner that night in March, I looked in on Donald as he sat on his mattress on the floor, writing in his journal. "Are you okay for the night?" I asked. "I'd like to sleep at my place tonight." He didn't look up at me, kept writing. "Yeah, sure. I'm okay." I walked home, leaving my VW camper parked in the lot across the alley from Donald's apartment. Home in my little studio, I did this and that, smoked a Camel and picked up a book to read. The phone rang. It was Pagan.

"Irma! Come quick! Something's happening with Donald!" "Okay. I'm coming."

As I walked the few blocks back, I had the awareness there was no need to hurry. I still had a key so I let myself in. Pagan, eyes large, so relieved to see me, just pointed at Donald's bedroom. I found him on his bed, bent over his oxygen machine, still hissing away. I turned it off. Felt for a heartbeat, a pulse. None. As I gently laid his body back down on the bed, I remembered what he'd said earlier that evening. "I broke one hundred today." Weighed less than one hundred pounds.

"Oh Donald," I breathed, aware that his spirit was in the room, watching—how well would I take care of Pagan? Aware too, that all the dreams I'd had of a loving life with him had now too expired.

I went to Pagan. I didn't tell her that her father had just died. "I have to call for an ambulance." How many times had I driven Donald to the Emergency at 3 or 4 in the morning? Leaving Pagan asleep. Getting her off to school when I returned. It took the Fire Department EMTs a few times around the block to find us, despite my very clear, concise instructions. The apartment was on a Walkway, half a block from the Pacific—one of the charming peculiarities of Venice Beach. Pagan and I watched them circling till they finally found us.

Two young men lifted Donald from his bed to the floor of the other room and proceeded to perform their heroics, pounding and punching his poor chest—to no avail.
I took Pagan out the kitchen door, where we sat on the steps, arms around each other. One man came and told Pagan that her father was dead. Now she cried as I held her. "He was coughing and coughing—it was awful!" she sobbed. "Then he yelled, 'Call Irma!'"

Police arrived, made phone calls to Kathy, Pagan's mother, in Norfolk, Virginia. She said she'd fly in the next day. They said Pagan would have to spend the night in a foster home because I was not a relative. After hours of phone calls, the manager of the foster home asked Kathy what she wanted for Pagan. Though we'd never met, nor even spoken, Kathy said she wanted Pagan to stay with me.

At some point in all the comings and goings of EMTs and policemen, of all the phone calls between police and Kathy and the foster care manager, somehow everyone was gone, even Pagan. I was alone with Donald's body as it lay on the floor, covered with a sheet. A day or two earlier I had given him over a hundred dollars, to help with his and Pagan's needs. He couldn't have spent it all and I felt I had a right to whatever he had left. Feeling nervous, fearful of someone walking in on me and thinking the worst, I searched his pockets. I found less than half of what I'd given him, but still a meaningful sum to me.

It was after one in the morning when they finally took his body to the morgue. It was cremated forty days later, on Walpurgisnacht, April 30, 1980. He had died on the first day of spring. His doctor had told me months before that Donald wouldn't last through the winter. Seems he was fiercely stubborn enough to prove the doctor wrong.

Pagan and I walked to my apartment around 2 A.M. When she woke in the morning, she said, "Irma, I had the most amazing dream of Donald! It was just as if he were alive! He was laughing and said to me, 'Well, wasn't that a big surprise! Didn't I fool you!'" Donald's attempt to comfort Pagan? We picked Kathy up at LAX late that morning—it was her birthday, and she was crying.

I hadn't cried yet, still in shock. A couple of days later, I took Pagan on an excursion to Capistrano, along with some residents of the Board and Care facility where I was the Recreation Director. There was a parade, a festival. I had a few moments alone, sitting by the Mission wall, watching the swallows return, saw an orange balloon drift into the sky. It felt like Donald, saying goodbye. The tears came then, and wouldn't stop.

Now is forever—
enduring loss/gain, praise/pain—
forever is Now.

<h1 style="text-align:center">Something in the Air</h1>

The first time I heard ABBA sing was in Venice Beach in 1980. Marti brought a tape from Ottawa when she came to visit in February. A present for me. I'd never heard them before—I could hear why she liked them so much.

A month later, after a long year of emphysema and labored breathing, Donald died—March 20—the first day of spring. His former wife, Kathy, and his son, Richard, came from the East coast to settle his things and to collect Pagan. We four got on well and were very busy for a week. Then they left and silence settled in.

Like the constant Pacific surf, waves of grief tumbled over me—dreams of adventure and pleasure with Donald—all gone. I listened to ABBA again and again. In the plaintive, inextinguishable longing in their voices I felt my own crumbled hopes and desperate desolation all rise to bursting. I had given up home, children, jobs and health in order to be with Donald. The harmonious voices of ABBA giving the lie to my life. I had loved him despite his anger and lust, and mine. Despite everything.

I heard ABBA sing, "...there was something in the air that night, Fernando..." and memory surged of how I'd met Donald on a park bench in Piraeus, Greece, our first dinner by the Mediterranean...A persistent, poignant note in that song wrung tears from my very being. Keening, I had to let go of any thought that Donald had truly loved me, though he once said he did—camping on the Peloponnesus in August, 1975, I'd said to him, "I can love you, Donald." And he'd said, "I can love you too." Now I wept. Dreams of love—all gone. The longing seemed to fade with the last notes of their song and a strange relief welled up inside me—I felt I'd laid those dreams to rest. I didn't know yet that I would dream of Donald for close to thirty years, absorbing what was good and releasing further need from my psyche bit by bit.

Still I felt adrift, a deep loss of life direction. I woke from an extraordinary dream one morning—an otter floating on its back in the ocean, opening a clam, washing and eating it in peace and contentment. I *knew* I was that otter! All was well. All would be well.

From Donald I had inherited a 'Don't Worry, Be Happy' poster of Meher Baba, a card with His picture, which I'd first seen in Donald's camper in Athens, and a book, *Listen, Humanity*. Things with which to start a new life—the scent of true love inherent in them.

In July 2018, I watched Cher sing "Fernando" and something writhed within me once again—belly contracted, tears came—for Irma of 1980— bereft, unmoored, alone. Days later, I listened again to ABBA sing "Fernando". No tears now. I am wept out, cleansed of that ancient grief. The promise of the Real Abba—Father —Meher Baba—fills the crevice of every need, and nurtures the longing for Him alone.

He Sings

— With respect to "The Mountain Song" by Buz Connor

Oh my love, don't go to the mountain.
Oh my love, don't go far away.
Stay, oh stay…

His voice leans into longing…
his tone rolls over hills of vast waves
seeming to end in the foreverness of gone.

Love lost—the list is long—
each one making ready room for the next deeper love,
daring my heart to hold more and more, again more.

Oh my love, don't go to the Ocean.
Oh my love, don't go to the Sea.
Wait for me…wait for me…

Plaintive echoes fade to sweet silence…
I rest in comfort on a gentle Ocean swell,
embrace the Love that quickens within.

In My Solitude

I woke up one day from a vivid dream, in which I saw an otter floating on its back, swishing an oyster or a clam and eating it. Floating on the gently swelling waves of the ocean. I knew in an instant that I was that otter—safe, sustained, well fed and cared for. I had nothing to worry about. That didn't entirely stop me from worrying, though. After all, I was wearing a neck brace because I'd injured my neck doing the plough yoga position at 5 A.M. some days ago. Still had lots of pain. I would look at the poster of Meher Baba at the foot of my built-in bed. *Don't Worry, Be Happy,* He said. I don't know how to do that, I said. I had not awakened yet to His Love…

I saw myself as bereft, washed up against the Pacific shore—in Venice Beach, the hippy-dippy part of Los Angeles. Donald, the man with whom I'd arrived there from Michigan, who had barely told me about Meher Baba and from whom I'd inherited this poster, had died just a month earlier, from emphysema. Shock and grief lingered. I'd helped to take care of him and Pagan. The day after he died, Pagan's mother, Kathy came from Norfolk, to deal with the formalities. Richard came from Boston. After a week they had all gone back East.

Alone and alone. I hardly knew what to do with myself. I'd been wrongfully fired from my Santa Monica job as a recreation director in a board and care home—that was a good thing, because my health and energy were ebbing low—now I was getting unemployment funds. My two children were in Illinois with their father and stepmother. In Venice I had no real friends. I was alone.

I lay on my built-into-the-wall bed and looked at Meher Baba in the poster. That's what it was—a poster. I read *Listen, Humanity* by Meher Baba and Don Stevens. I wanted to believe Baba was who he said he was. That's where I was—wanting him to be that, as I read his words.

Just the same, the dream of the otter seemed so real that it helped me through that day and the next and the next…I don't know how long it was before one day, in the silence of that pleasant studio apartment, there came a moment in my solitude when I suddenly *knew, just knew!* that Meher Baba was Who He said He was—God in human form. The Avatar! For weeks I was inexplicably joyful. Like an otter.

Cocooned like caterpillars
we abide in semi-seclusion with Him—
He's naturally having His way within us and
in His time, He will spring us loose—
awakening to His love,
ready to fly!

Eyes of Kindness

As I was first reading *Listen, Humanity* shortly before I came to Meher Baba, I was taken by the clarity of Don Stevens' writing. I found myself wanting to believe that Meher Baba was who he said he was. A few weeks later I had the experience of *knowing* that Baba was Who He said He was—God in human form.

Later in July 1980, Don was a guest speaker at the Southern California *sahavas*. Listening to Don, I was struck by his implicit obedience to Meher Baba both in his personal and professional life. I have never forgotten his description of how he would "report" to Baba at the end of each day—speaking to Baba out loud. In the years since, I have often reported to Baba on my daily walks.

In 2003, my husband Karl and I invited Don to come to our home in Tucson to do a weekend presentation on his latest book, *Meher Baba's Word & His Three Bridges*. Having picked him up at the airport, I told Don how I'd read *Listen, Humanity,* wanting to believe, and how a few days or weeks later, I'd had the total experience of *knowing* that Meher Baba was God in human form. Don said to me, "So you experienced the Presence of the Master!" I was taken aback. I'd never thought of it that way, yet it expressed my experience as I never could. It certainly explained the unexpected, unprecedented joy I'd felt for weeks and months afterward.

I could see, over that weekend in 2003, that Don's knees were weak, but his presentation was not. Forthright, clear, concise, authoritative. Baba lovers from all over southern Arizona flocked in, eager to see and hear Don speak. We learned about the three bridges to God.

A few years later, Karl and I began to hear about the Beads-on-One-String pilgrimages Don was leading in India. In 2010 we knew it was time to go on that year's pilgrimage. We arrived in New Delhi a few days early to allow for jet lag to run its course. It happened that Don had arrived early as well. Meeting him in the dining room unexpectedly, and despite feeling shy as I usually did with the *mandali,* we shared a warm greeting. What stayed with me forever afterward were his eyes of kindness. It didn't matter that for the next week or so, he called me Irene. It was in Hyderabad that I whispered into his ear, "My name is Irma." Don asked if I could forgive him. With a smile, I said I'd give it some thought, counting on his wry sense of humor.

Karl and I emailed back and forth with Don after the pilgrimage was over and we were back in Tucson. I sent him a photo or two, and a poem I'd written. Don sent us an email saying, "Karl and Irma can do no wrong." We were thrilled, even after someone told us that he said this to all his companions.

When Don passed on early in 2011, some months after a fall while in France, I felt happy for him—he had spent most of his life in service to his Master, Meher Baba—he had served Baba well.

To this day I can see Don in my mind's eye, as he looked on our 2010 Beads-on-One String pilgrimage all over India. I can hear his voice—steady, calm. I was delighted to read that Baba had said to Eruch two or three times, in front of Don, that Don was a *mandali*. Baba also said that Don was an example of a near perfect balance of head and heart.

Can I imagine Him
looking at me with such Love?
His Love!
This thought startles my heart
into the depths of longing.

My First Dhuni—Ready to Take a Step

I went to my first Baba meeting on Friday, June 13, 1980 in Los Angeles. One day a month or so before, after reading *Listen, Humanity,* I had experienced Meher Baba's Presence, and He gave me to know He was God. At the meetings I heard about the July 4th Silence Day *Sahavas* —there'd be a *dhuni* there. I'd read about the *dhuni* in *Listen, Humanity*—I could throw into the fire something I want to give up. I knew I had to go to this *sahavas*, to throw smoking into the *dhuni*. It was the only way I could stop smoking.

I'd been smoking since I was fourteen and had been trying to stop, especially since Donald, my Baba contact had just died of emphysema. I got down to one cigarette a day—the one that helped me get to sleep. One day I didn't smoke at all. That night I didn't sleep at all. The next day I didn't smoke, and again I didn't sleep. After 3 A.M. I panicked and ran down to the liquor store and bought a pack of unfiltered Camels. That really scared me—to be that dependent on cigarettes.

I drove to the Southern California Silence Day *Sahavas* at the Pilgrim Pines church camp in the San Bernardino Mountains. On the last evening of the *sahavas*, I felt thrills wash through me as we watched the new film, "O Parvardigar," the first time I saw Meher Baba in motion. Then we walked in silence to the open area where there was a fire pit. We said the "O Parvardigar " prayer as the

dhuni was lit. I watched carefully to see what these fol-
lowers of Meher Baba did here—they bowed down,
touched their foreheads to casts of Baba's feet. Would I
bow down to His feet? A new way of knowing myself.

One by one, after a moment of concentration, they threw
a stick of sandalwood into the fire. As I watched, I pon-
dered—would I throw in just cigarettes…or all smoking,
including dope—marijuana. The mind's last minute ef-
fort to bargain. Then it was time to get into line and after
several minutes, I found myself ready to take the steps
toward His feet, toward the *dhuni*. Sandalwood stick in
hand, I laid my forehead at His feet.

Threw all smoking into the fire!

Meher Baba said that the *dhuni* has the power of a saint,
and it indeed took away from me all desire to smoke. I
never again felt the urge or the need for a cigarette. I am
eternally grateful. My first night home after the *sahavas*, I
didn't know how to get into bed without my bedtime
smoke. I turned around and around in small circles, like a
dog getting ready to lie down. I felt very strange, disoriented. Could it be that in throwing smoking into the
dhuni, a lifetime of habits had also been shaken up?

The future is next,
And yet it is always now—
Now, trusting in You.

Coming to Baba

It was Filis Frederick in the summer of 1980, who first asked me how I came to Baba. I don't remember if she used that exact phrase, and it being the first time I was asked, I was shy and had a sparse response for her and the Baba lovers gathered in her Hermosa Beach home for her Monday Night meeting. I must have said something about Donald and *Listen, Humanity,* but I don't remember what else I said.

It was perhaps six months later that Eruch asked me how I came to be sitting in Mandali Hall, Meherazad. I must have heard a few people relate their coming to Baba stories since I'd arrived in India on January 3rd, 1981, and perhaps, despite my shyness, I had more of a story to tell. It probably started with meeting Donald, whom I saw as my Baba-contact. Did I tell Eruch and the gathered Baba lovers that I'd sold my VW camper in Los Angeles, and having nothing else to do with my life, nowhere else to go and knowing that my life was not in L.A., I used that money for a ticket to India because I kept hearing about *Amartithi,* which seemed to have meaning for my life.

While I don't remember what all I said, I must have mentioned that moment when I experienced Baba, *Real within me,* in my studio apartment in Venice Beach. All this in the self-consciousness and curious mixture of wanting to tell about myself and wanting to disappear.

What I remember now is how I was sitting on my bed, thinking about my life with Donald, who had just died—how I had not been the love of his life, and the beginning admission to myself that he too had not been the love of mine either. Something freeing in that moment—the recognition of that as an evanescent dream—and letting it go. I think now that that letting go allowed me to experience the Real moment with Meher Baba soon after. Knowing Meher Baba as the Real Love of my life.

In the ten years that elapsed until my next pilgrimage to Meherabad with my daughter, I'd moved to Tucson, married Karl and became acquainted with the Southern Arizona Baba lovers. I probably heard the question and responses more than once—how did you come to Meher Baba? Stephanie and I spent two months in Meherabad in 1991. Nana Kher would sit with the two of us and ask us how we came to Baba. After we had said two or three sentences, Nana Kher would intersperse an anecdote, a memory, or a saying and then we would go on with our stories. In this way, it took several days for us to finish telling our stories, because, all of a sudden the bell would ring for 4 o'clock tea, and none of us wanted to miss that!

And during tea or walking up the Hill for *arti*, details would come to me—this had happened only after that had occurred. So the next afternoon with Nan Kher, I'd elaborate on my story, starting it earlier and earlier in my life, and Nan Kher would weave in his stories and then it would be tea time again. By the third day, Stephanie pointed out to me how I kept changing my story. I protested that I was recognizing how my story had begun further and further back in my life. When and where did I start seeking God?

If, as Eruch said as Baba had said, that those of us who had come to Baba but had never seen Him in His body, had seen Him face to face in our previous lives, then it only made sense that I'd been seeking Baba all my life… but when did I first become conscious of that? Have I always been 'coming' to Baba?

In my story I tell about my conviction during my Lutheran confirmation classes that I would be altered after I had had my first communion. I did experience an altered state of consciousness later that year, in which I knew I was not 'Irma', not this identity. But I remember an earlier time at thirteen when I prayed to God for the first time in my life with all my heart—trying to reach God—begging for help, knowing that only He could help me. I did receive that help, though I didn't recognize it as such for decades.

In my awareness of myself as 'Irma' in the body I recognize a number of steps, events, one leading to another, a series of breadcrumbs, that culminate in a moment of knowing Meher Baba is God, is the Avatar. Internally, there is a less documented series of awarenesses of myself in relation to God, of God's presence within me. These two sets of awarenesses are interwoven in a saga of compelling unfolding—sometimes rapid, sometimes in agonizing slow motion.

But Baba says He is always with us, within us, each of us—so what is the 'coming'? Or does Baba 'come' to us? He is always what is Real in us, so what could the 'coming' be? I recently reread a quote of Baba's, which suddenly answered my question.

"When the Word of My Love breaks out of its Silence and speaks in your hearts, telling you Who I really am, you will know that that is the Real Word you have always been longing to hear."

That Kind of Love

I read a line from Rumi.
Tears come—my old habit
upon recognizing truth—
that or laugh.

There's nothing else to do.
Being seen
with that kind of love,
I cannot hold the mask.

Filis and Me

The gentle love in Filis's voice and in her smile have stayed with me to this day. I can see her without closing my eyes. I can hear her voice caressing Baba's name.

On the last evening of the 1980 Los Angeles Sahavas, I threw smoking into the *dhuni*—and it did indeed take from me all desire to smoke. But a month later I found myself on a hippie farm in San Luis Obispo, my companions there smoking joints of home grown dope. I looked wistful, so they consoled me, saying there were brownies in the freezer. I didn't take one until the next day, when they were all gone and I was at total loose ends. I didn't get high, but slogged through the day wandering about the farm, feeding their goats wild anise and cleaning their kitchen. Still feeling infinitely vague, I finally just went to bed.

A few days later, at Filis's Monday night meeting in Hermosa Beach, I heard her say that Meher Baba had said, "No recreational drugs." A wash of relief came over me—I need never be tempted again by dope in any form—this temptation forever taken from me!

I was desperately lonely living by myself in Venice Beach. Before coming to Baba, I'd have gone to the boardwalk and found a man to mess with. Now I didn't always know what to do with myself. It was years before I recognized how Baba emptied my life, shaking family, friends, lovers, jobs, bad habits and more out of it, like dirty laundry. Years before I could appreciate the value and blessing of that. Making room for His Love.

As I read Henry Miller's books, where he described his primitive watercolor paintings, I decided to try that too. I made a crude booklet of watercolor paintings with writing at the bottom of each page, describing how desperately I wanted a friend. A woman or a man—tall or short, young, old, thin, fat—or even a cat. I have no idea what inspired me to show this to Filis, But I did—I left it with her. A few weeks later, she returned it to me. I saw and felt the kindness in her eyes and in her voice as she handed it back to me, thanking me for letting her see it. In retrospect, I think showing her this booklet was one of the most courageous things I've ever done.

In the summer of 1981 I was staying at a friend's house in Detroit, after a two and a half month stay in Meherabad, India. I contacted Detroit area Baba lovers, Mike Leever and Buck Busfield. We heard Filis would be in Chicago, and agreed to drive there and back in one day. After Filis's talk I went to chat with her, to let her know about my time in India. She seemed pleased to see me, and told me news from Los Angeles—this one had married that one, and that one had married this one. "You should come back and get married there too," she told me.

I had so much love and respect for Filis, and yet I could not imagine returning to Los Angeles. I had left because

I'd had a strong intuition that my life was not there. I thanked her, saying I'd give it some thought. It turned out that I did eventually go way west to be married, but to Tucson, not Los Angeles—a different kind of desert. Thirty-seven years later I dreamt of Filis:

Seeing Filis come toward me,
I stand to greet her,
feel the warmth
of our full-hearted embrace,
cheek to cheek with love.
We step apart—
a flash of *oneness* from eye to eye
fills my heart.

"Is He Coming Back?"

"Is anyone free and able to take me to see Jean Adriel?" he asked. British accent. The Los Angeles Baba meeting on Santa Monica Blvd. had just ended and Baba lovers were getting up from their seats. The British man stood near the front of the room—I don't remember if I'd noticed him before, but I was noticing him now—a good-looking guy. I was free. I was able. "I can do that," I spoke up quickly, not wanting to lose this opportunity to get to know him and to meet Jean Adriel. Her book, *Avatar,* was the second book about Baba I had bought and read, the first being *Listen, Humanity* by Don Stevens.

It was late August 1980. I was an almost brand new Baba baby, having been graced by His Presence a few months earlier, perhaps in April. I'd faithfully attended Baba meetings since my first on Friday, June 13th—that became my lucky day! And I'd spent three memorable days at the Southern California July 4th *Sahavas*

I introduced myself to this man, learned his name, exchanged phone numbers and he gave me his address. Keith was from London, visiting L.A. I was at such loose ends in my life that this outing was a gift to me. Donald had died on the first day of spring that year, I'd lost my job as recreation director at a board and care home and was living on unemployment funds and whatever interesting short term jobs I could find. A lot of empty, lost-feeling space in between.

I picked Keith up and headed north on I-5. My 1972 VW poptop camper did not have air-conditioning, so our windows were open—still not cool enough for Keith — not used to Southern California summer heat. He was perspiring and being from London, he hadn't thought to bring water for himself. We were early for visiting hours at the nursing home where Jean was staying and had to somehow pass an hour or more. Keith asked if we could stop for refreshments. "Sure." I took us to Van Nuys north of L.A., where my friend, Norm's, former brother-in-law, my former dope dealer and his Hispanic wife, Stella, lived. I knew she'd be home and happy to see us. And she was—gave us cool drinks as we chatted an hour away. Back in the camper, Keith remarked, "One can see the difficulties and challenges of being beautiful." It gave me pause. Stella was beautiful and his comment shone a light into her life that I hadn't perceived before. Trading on beauty for social acceptance and economic security does not, in fact, enhance self-esteem.

We stopped to buy cookies and chocolates to bring along, arrived at the nursing home and were shown to Jean's room. After introducing ourselves, we brought out the treats. Jean seemed pleased with our company. Keith asked about her times with Baba. I was so new to Baba, I hardly knew to have any questions. Jean was in her 90s, frail in body and mind, but totally present and coherent as she related one story after another—her precious times with Baba. I do not now remember any of them.

What I do clearly remember is how, after telling us her stories, Jean looked at us beseechingly and asked, over and over, *"Is He coming back? Is He really coming back?"* Her utmost concern. We assured her that He was indeed coming back. What else could we say? Besides, He said He was coming back, so it must be true. Her intense questions now cause me to think she felt haunted by something unfinished, unresolved in her relationship with Meher Baba, and she desperately wanted Him to come back so it could be resolved. I may never know.

After half an hour or so, Jean began to wander mentally. She declined more treats and shifted around on her bed, seemed to lose awareness of our presence—she'd come back for a moment, then be gone again. An aide stepped into the room and suggested Jean was tired now, that we should depart. We agreed and said goodbye and Jai Meher Baba, to which Jean responded. And we left.

As I drove Keith home, he talked about how much he loved avocados—so plentiful in Los Angeles—and how he ate them every day during his visit. He was engaging and a pleasure to be with. I'd been intensely lonely and longed for more time with him. It felt like I'd been cloistered in Donald's illness and was now blissing out on the sunlight of normal conversation. How to tell someone about life with a dying man? I didn't.

At our next Baba meeting I was pleased to see Keith again. He shared details of our visit with Jean with the group. At the meeting's end, I went to say goodbye to Keith. I remember he said, "You don't look long for staying here. Come to England!" Before the year was out, I was on my way to India via London.

Ocean

Sometimes this thunderous Lover
sprays me with foam.

Sometimes this mellifluous Friend
entreats me, *come Home.*

He Turned the Key

My journey from Venice Beach in Los Angeles to Poona, India took me first to Detroit for a few weeks, staying with my friend, Norm—setting the stage for eventually meeting my future husband, Karl, then on to London, where I stayed in Pete Townshend's Boathouse for six days, spent New Year's Eve with Keith and his friends, then a flight to Delhi and Bombay, and finally a second class seat on a train to Poona.

Baba lovers in L.A. recommended that I stay overnight in Poona to rest and meet Jal, Meher Baba's brother. They also recommended I stay at the National Hotel across the road from the Poona railway station. It was owned and run by Baha'i people, they said, who were friendly to Baba lovers. So when the train stopped I picked up my backpack and daypack, got off the train relieved to see the hotel across the road. I had written to the Trust in Ahmednagar saying I would come for Baba's Amartithi, but I'd had no reply. Part of me wondered if they'd let me in or if there'd be "no room at the inn." I'd have gone an awfully long way to find that out! And I had no place to go back to—I'd completely cleared out of Venice.

I entered the hotel, approached the counter, set down my backpack. "I'd like a room for one night, please," I said to the tall man behind the counter. "I have no room," he said. What!? I couldn't fathom the challenge of finding another hotel on my own. Too many hours in the air, on

the bus, the train…I just stood there. "No room?" I echoed bleakly, looking as dazed as I felt.

"Are you coming from Ahmednagar?"
"No," I said. "I'm going there."
"And I suppose you want to see Jal too?"
"Oh yes," I stammered. "If that is possible."

After another glance at my jeans, my backpack, my long
hair, he turned to the cubbyholes behind him and picked
a key from one. Turning to me, he said, "There is one
room," and offered me the key. I needed a moment to put
all this together—I'd passed a test. I knew the secret
words, the right people. I was not a Rajneeshee —not
wearing orange or red. Did he sift through all strangers
like this, I wondered, weeding out some and not others.

I fell into my mosquito-netted bed—a first—and slept
like the dead for three hours. Awoke in time for tea in the
lobby —where Jal found me, shouting, "Where is this girl
who is so afraid?" Baba had turned the key!

Only He

We say whatever we can,
We try whatever we can,
We do everything we can,

but only He
can turn the key.

190

I Feel Such Compassion for You

The first time I spoke with Mani, Meher Baba's sister, was on the Mandali Hall veranda at Meherazad, India in the first week of January 1981. In Poona, the day before, her brother, Jal, had told me to convey some thousands of love greetings to her from himself. I recognized the sweetness this allowed me in my first meeting with Mani. She in turn, told me to return a similar number of love greetings to Jal, when I should next see him. I guessed this was a favorite amusing, yet loving ploy to usher in new and even old lovers of Baba to the *mandali* in Meherazad and Meherabad.

Weeks later in February, Eruch was telling us stories in Mandali Hall. As she sometimes did, Mani slipped in and sat on the carpet, near me this time. She may have added an anecdote or vignette as she sat amongst us. But it was in a silent moment, no one talking, when she looked at me and very quietly said, *I feel such compassion for you.*

Stunned, I looked at her. Said nothing. How to take this? Not a moment to ask questions and receive answers. My mind flashing through the myriad losses, grief and traumas in my life, I gave a small nod to acknowledge what she had said. Everything that had happened in my life served in some way to bring me here to this place, in this moment—to receive acknowledgment for my pain, from Baba, perhaps, through His dear sister.

I had forgotten this moment until recently, and wonder now if perhaps it was connected to another moment with Mani in July 1991. Mani and I were sitting on Mehera's porch, just the two of us. *Wie geht es Ihnen? How are you?* she asked. She would have known I was German-born from my passport, and may have wanted to practice her German. But somehow, hearing her German words hit me hard. I exploded into tears. *Oh Mani, it was awful! Awful!!* I gasped and wept uncontrollably, flooded with memories of pain and ugliness, of need and desire, of force and seduction, of anxiety and anger, of lies and threats and shame and more—all in my family…A long moment she sat with me. I don't remember if she said anything as I wept.

A young family with two small children came up on the porch. Mani went to greeted them and began to play with the children. I choked back my tears, knowing my face was flaming with grief and shame. She had walked away from me, giving her full attention to the children now. While part of me could understand this—she had gracefully given me space to collect myself—yet a young part of me felt abandoned and ashamed for my outburst. So exposed, I never felt able to approach Mani after that.

In all the years since, whenever I read about Mani or heard someone talk about how wonderful she was, I knew what they meant—I saw and felt that too. But I was never able to understand what had happened in that moment. Did I do something shameful in losing control of myself, when Mani had simply wanted a bit of chat in German? Or was this Baba's way of releasing a flood of grief in a flash, with Mani as the catalyst?

I have no doubt that everything that happens is for my benefit, so I have to believe Baba arranged this as a release for me. Ten years before, Mani had already said to me, in front of everyone, *I feel such compassion for you.*

Your Love

lays its gentle hand upon my arm,
leads me on the only path
my heart can bear

On the Way Down the Hill

I was a new Baba lover, less than a year old, when I stayed in Meherabad for the first time early in 1981. Meeting Baba's *mandali* was astounding. I saw how other Baba lovers felt so close to one or another of them —Mehera or Mani, Eruch, Pendu or Padri—keen in their delight. And though I listened closely and observed intensely each of Baba's *mandali* at every chance, I didn't felt *close* to any of them.

One day, feeling troubled about this apparent lack of connection as I walked down the Hill after morning *arti*, I remembered Don Stevens talking about reporting out loud to Baba. This seemed like a good time for that, so I spoke to Baba.

"Baba, so many of Your lovers here have such a close relationship with one or another of Your *mandali*, but I don't feel that kind of closeness with any of them."

Baba responded immediately within myself,
"The only relationship that counts is the one with Me!"

Can you imagine my relief and my gratitude?!

In Your Eyes

The light you see in my eyes
is Baba peeking out
to see if He can see Himself
in your eyes.

Chinese Medicine

In the 1980s I used to go to the Tucson Gem Show with Meff Thompson, who had a small import shop on Fourth Avenue, so she could get us wholesale prices on anything we bought. I fell in love with lapis lazuli—its celestial blue intensity intact from the mountains of Afghanistan. I bought handfuls of lapis beads in different sizes, along with red cinnabar beads from China, including two tiny enameled cinnabar horses. I bought a necklace-making tray so I could figure out how to arrange the beads with one of the horses. I wanted the horse at one side of the necklace, so I had to find a way to counter that weight and to visually balance the other side of the necklace. I played with the beads' arrangement for days and weeks until I had what I wanted.

One day I wore the necklace to our Food Buying Club meeting. A woman there asked me where I'd gotten that necklace. I'd heard she had some psychic abilities, so her interest caught my attention. I told her I'd made it myself, that the beads and all were from the Gem Show. She gave me a long look. Why? I asked. She hesitated for just a beat, then said, *That is an exact replica of a necklace you wore long ago as a Chinese healer.* I probably just said, Oh. But I've never forgotten that moment—I can still picture where we stood, in her kitchen just off of Swan Road.

For the past few months I've been receiving dry needle acupuncture from the husband and wife team at The Alternative Clinic here in Asheville, North Carolina, where we now live. It's been the first truly effective treatment for my left leg since I fell on it in September. 2017 They are also prescribing Chinese herbs for my digestion, for strengthening my heart and for herpes, which has been with me since childhood.

The fall in September seemed at first inconvenient, then painful, causing sleep disturbance for months, and cost more dollars than I care to tell, as I tried this and that remedy or procedure. It has now proved to be an instigator toward deeper healing in my so-called old age.

I look at the miscellanea of herbs they give me to make into tea—barks, berries, mushrooms, twigs—and I think of the thousands of years it took to identify the uses of each, by intuition, by trial and error. Perhaps I was a part of that process. Only now in my maturity am I ready to receive the benefits of Chinese medicine.

Before we left Tucson I sold half or more of my jewelry—I never wear it anymore—but I did keep this lapis necklace, remembering what that woman said. It's an exact replica of one I wore long, long ago as a Chinese healer. No wonder it took me so long to figure out exactly how to place the tiny horse and each bead.

The Distance between Us

The last time I watched a movie with Alex was on Christmas Day, 1986 in Tucson. Alex had come from Michigan to spend his holidays with us. On Christmas Day we drove up Mt. Lemmon, had an early dinner there, then came back to town to watch "Out of Africa," which had just come out with Meryl Streep and Robert Redford, two of my favorite actors.

Karl and I were renting a house on Prospect Lane then, in Polly Lee's compound near the Rillito River. Alex was on the verge of eighteen—his birthday was on January 15th. He was tall, 6'3", taller than either his father or me, almost as tall as Karl. Karl let Alex ride his Norton motorcycle, which was probably a bit too heavy for him to handle well, but he managed. One day we took Alex on a hike in Pima Canyon with our friend, Robert Frost, all making silly jokes about "The Christmas Chicken." Another day we went to the Racquet Club, where Karl and Alex played racquetball and we soaked in the jacuzzi. I wanted Alex to look at a comet through a telescope at the Flandreau Planetarium, so we stood in line for it, but it turned out to be too cloudy, and the evening was a dud.

I was having a hard time connecting with Alex on an intimate level. So I filled our time with fun things to do. Too many years apart. He'd been living with his dad in Illinois and in Michigan for nine years, and I'd only seen him when he was thirteen—he came to Norfolk, Virginia for a week in the summer of 1982. I'd had a hard time connecting with him then too. At the Norfolk airport I was walking toward the arrival area when a tall young man almost passed by me, and suddenly said, "Mom?" I'm sure I blinked. Hard. Alex! He was taller than me! Five years since I'd seen him. Maybe that's when the distance between us showed up. How to close the gap of five preadolescent years? We tried.

Pagan helped a lot—she was twelve and very outgoing. I took them to Virginia Beach—a water slide, the ocean. We sailed on a ship I'd done some painting on. We found a grey kitten, Felix, at a pet shop. We made granola and clam chowder, which Alex didn't care for, especially after he'd cut his finger as we opened the clams. I've long regretted that.

I gave Alex my room at Kathy's and I slept on the sofa. One evening we sat on the front porch and tried to convey our lives to each other. He told me about Boy Scouts, football and a girlfriend. I told him about Meher Baba and India. He told me about Dungeons and Dragons and air guitar. I told him about Venice Beach. There was a lot in my life that I wasn't going to tell my thirteen-year-old son, whom I hadn't seen in five years. Five years that were wider and often choppier than the Atlantic.

Almost five years later, in Tucson, he was even taller—*too tall*, he said. I didn't understand how an eighteen-year-old boy could be too tall. (As a girl in the '50s, early '60s, I was too tall at 5'10". Most boys were shorter and the arms and legs of girls' clothes were always too short for me.) But for a boy?

He was smoking—we asked him to smoke on the patio or the front porch. I watched as he walked to the corner store for cigarettes, looking singularly alone—as I felt—not being able to be the mom I used to be to my little boy. The boy I'd read good night stories to, making funny voices for the characters. I'd kiss his cheek and take in the little boy scent of his hair. And he'd say, "Kiss me on the wips, Mom. Kiss me on the wips!"

On the first day of kindergarten, a little girl had followed him home." She's my girlfriend," he said. "Can I keep her?" After school once, he barged through the back door, jumped up the two steps into the kitchen and shouted, "Guess what Mom! Wanna hear a dirty joke?" "Okay..." "A dog fell into a mud puddle!" He jumped around and laughed and giggled. I laughed too, mostly out of relief.

After Alex's visit in Norfolk, I took him to the airport. We hugged and kissed goodbye. In the parking lot, I watched his plane soar across the sky—and had the sudden premonition of his early and violent death. *I just knew!* It *shook* me. Tears came hot and fast. No matter how much I wanted to, I could *not* not know what I knew then. There was nothing I could do but pray to Baba, again and again. His response always was the same—*Don't worry, be happy. I have taken care of everything.* I would put Alex into His hands and try to obey His order.

Christmas Day 1986, we sat together and watched "Out of Africa" in Tucson. I had forgotten almost all of that story until Karl and I watched it again on Monday, December 24th, 2018, thirty-two years later. "I once had a farm in Africa..." Meryl Streep reminisces in the film. And I think, "I once had a son who thought he was too tall..."

Sometimes the tears still come.

Infinite Care

When tears come
she dabs
with infinite care
beneath her eyes.

No one ever told me not to,
so I rubbed mine.

When she reaches my age,
she will look still young,
while I will look
merely wise.

Near Ecstasy

When I want to picture Baba, an image comes easily to mind, taken in 1954 at the Kushroo Quarters *darshan*, where He is seated, leaning forward, His hands cupping the cheeks of a small Indian boy, who stands still, eye to eye with Baba, enthralled, while his two older sisters stand behind him, one holding his shoulders as if to keep him from falling into Baba, smiling, laughing, unable to contain their joy at seeing their dear little brother so blessed with Baba's hands—His smile not only on His lips, but also in His luminous unworldly eyes—the love, the thrilling delight passing through the boy, into the girls, one by one, till one cannot maintain her normal posture and collapses onto her sister in utter delight — sister holding sister holding brother—Baba's loving touch holding them all—a chain of near ecstasy, a charged moment held forever in their memory and mine.

A Rainy Afternoon

The last time I was together with both my daughter Stephanie, twenty-one and my son Alex, eighteen, was in June 1987 in Royal Oak, Michigan, in my stepmother's apartment. I had flown from Tucson to Michigan for Stephanie's graduation from community college. Alex, too, had just graduated high school. One morning, Stephanie drove them from Lake Orion, where they lived with their father, to Royal Oak, taking along their twelve-year-old half-sister, Danielle.

We walked around downtown Royal Oak, just blocks away from Luella's place, looking for graduation gifts—luggage for Stephanie and Birkenstocks for Alex. Later, in August of that year, Stephanie used her luggage to come live with Karl and me in Tucson. We didn't find the right Birks so I ended up getting Alex a Samsonite duffel bag. He told me later on the phone that he used the bag to carry his Dungeons & Dragons stuff when he went to play with his friends. I had hoped, of course, that he too would use it one day to travel to Arizona again.

It was cloudy and on the verge of drizzle as we headed back to Luella's. Dad was there too, visiting from the nursing home where he now lived, just a few blocks away. We piled into Luella's sedan and headed to a nearby pizza place for lunch. Dad was treating us. I'd told the kids earlier that if he offered them any money, to not take it, because he had only enough on him for our lunch. Dad had long had the habit of handing out fives, tens, even twenties and senile dementia didn't stop him from still doing that.

We sat around a large table—Stephanie with long golden bronze curls and Alex six foot, three, one on each side of me. Dad suddenly advised Stephanie, "Stay with him—he's a good man." We were all startled into silence, looking at each other. Dad's dementia. We let it go. Even if we'd reminded him that they were sister and brother, he'd have forgotten in the next instant. It must have really surprised Danielle too.

The drizzle had become a regular rainy afternoon as we scurried back into Luella's apartment. How to entertain ourselves now? What to do? I remembered *Pobby*, a book we had when Stephanie and Alex were younger. It gave the numbers from 1 to 10 new names I'd never forgotten. I recited them with a flourish: *ounce, dice, trice, quartz, quince, sego, septum, oxygen, nitrogen, denim*. My kids remembered and their faces lit up. Luella looked intrigued, Dad and Danielle were clueless, out of the loop. *Let's make up new names for the rest of the numbers*. A few eyebrows went up, a glint of interest.

What new name shall we give for eleven? Stephanie, then Alex threw out a few words…interest revved up and soon we had it: *elf*. A nod to German.

When Stephanie was eleven, she and Donald, my fellow adventurer and I left Ferndale, in my VW pop-top camper, and camped across the country, ending up in Venice Beach five months later. It was truly wonderful to see so many events and natural wonders: Pipestone National Monument in Minnesota, the Black Hills (Paha Sapa) and the Badlands in South Dakota, the Green River dinosaur excavation, a pow-wow at Fort Duchene, Arches National Park and Hovenweep Canyon in Utah, the Grand Canyon, the Snake Dance and other sacred festivals on the Hopi Mesas in Arizona, the redwoods in northern California, and more. A magnificent education for Stephanie and me—more than she could have gotten from the last week of fifth grade that she missed in Ferndale, and the two months of sixth grade she missed in Venice Beach.

The difficult parts were due the fact that she and Donald did not easily get along, and I was in the middle, sometimes taking one side, sometimes the other—comfortable with neither, and sometimes staying out of it. I lost ten pounds and began to have painful outbreaks on my skin. Donald's comment was that it may be the plague, since outbreaks had occurred on some reservations. Whether he was being funny or serious, I didn't appreciate it. It wasn't that plague, but a stress-induced autoimmune condition that has plagued me on and off to this day.

When Alex was eleven, he was living with his father, Cliff, stepmother, Christine and half-sister, Danielle in Illinois. There were times when I ached to see him, chat with him, listen to one of his kid jokes.

The giddy suggestions for twelve made it clear that this was a project for Stephanie, Alex and me. Luella in the kitchen, making tea, pouring juice. Dad about to doze off on the sofa. Danielle clambering in and out of a large cardboard box, opening and closing an umbrella. We found our way to a new twelve—*doze!*

For Stephanie's twelfth birthday in March 1978, Mimi, the lunch chef at Chez Helene, where I worked, treated us to a private lunch and gave Stephanie a lovely comb for her long, still blonde curly hair. Donald, in a dour mood, disapproved of all this attention given to her, though his daughter, Pagan, 7, thoroughly enjoyed it all.

Soon after, Stephanie broke her right arm climbing up a doorjamb and falling—something she'd already done once in Ferndale. For some weeks I helped her with homework, writing down her answers for her. I realized that Venice and our life there were not the best for Stephanie, though she'd gotten into the accelerated Gates program at school. We talked about it and agreed that she would go live with her Dad and Alex in June when she'd finished sixth grade. Heartache at LAX, letting her go too. Empty nest at thirty-four!

Thirteen became *trinket*.

At thirteen, Stephanie sent me letters; Alex rarely. But once when he wrote, I suddenly recognized that his handwriting was exactly like mine—I couldn't tell the difference! I took it to mean that we had a strong, true inner connection. When Alex was thirteen, I was living in Norfolk, Virginia with Kathy Hill, Donald's former wife and their daughter, Pagan. (Donald had died of emphysema in March 1980.) I was home-schooling Pagan for sixth grade. I invited Alex to come visit us in July 1982. We had a week of fun events: the Atlantic shore and water slides at Virginia Beach, sailing on a ship I'd done some painting on, pizza, finding a grey kitten we named Felix. One evening Alex and I had some quiet time on the front porch, but I found it very difficult to bridge the gap of five years since I'd last seen him. He'd grown so much—he was taller than me. In fact, when I'd gone to the airport to pick him up I didn't know his plane had come in early, and I was about to walk past him in the corridor, when he said, "Mom?" I was shocked I hadn't immediately recognized him—I was remembering an eight-year-old boy.

A week later, I took Alex back to the airport—we said, "I love you…goodbye." Some minutes later I stood in the parking lot, watching his plane soar overhead. And suddenly I *knew*....a precognition of his early and violent death. I knew, and could never again *not* know.

On a roll now, the teens rattled around the room and came out as *froze, quizzle, sizzle, september, october, november.* And twenty was now *vinegar*—a nod to French.

Through Stephanie's teen years she sent me letters, photos, a small gift I still cherish—it came at a time in Venice when I was keenly missing my children. I used to visualize Stephanie and Alex, surround them with white light, send them love. It brought me some peace. Years later, she told me she was sitting alone in their living room in Lake Orion when suddenly the room was filled with love and light. I read her letters eagerly—her plans for archery, for travel to Europe, for college. Monthly phone conversations. She told me about her boyfriend.

Stephanie was fourteen when I first flew to India, to Meherabad to visit Meher Baba's Tomb. I bought several small things at the Ahmednagar bazaar for her and Alex, put wrapped candies on Baba's Tomb—*prasad* to send to them. I wanted them to know about Meher Baba. It would be delicate. She told me later that she'd asked Alex if he wanted any of the candy. He said no, so she had it all. At seventeen she visited us in Tucson. Later, I sent her a copy of the first Meher Baba calendar.

Alex was seventeen, almost eighteen when he visited us in Tucson over his Christmas vacation in 1986. We hiked in the Catalina Mountains, made jokes about getting presents from 'the Christmas Chicken' instead of Santa, saw "Out of Africa" on Christmas Day. He was six foot, three and smoking. He thought he was too tall. I remembered smoking at fourteen, joking it might stunt my growth. Karl let him ride his Norton motorcycle. I still didn't have enough time with him to bridge the growing gap from the boy I'd known. We invited him to come live with us, go to University. He said he'd think about it.

Early Friday evening, September 18, 1987, our phone rang. It was Cliff's Aunt Ruby calling for Stephanie. A moment later she crumpled into tears. Handed me the phone and it was my turn. A thirty-one year-old man, high on alcohol and Valium, crossed the centerline of a Michigan highway in his big Lincoln—crashed head on into Alex in his VW Rabbit. Not wearing a seatbelt, Alex was thrown from his car and died instantly (I have always been grateful for this). This is what the doctor at the Michigan hospital told me a few hours later. Alex was eighteen. I remembered how as a little kid, one of his favorite games was to play "smash 'em up" with his Matchbox cars. I had always thought I'd have more time again with Alex.

This event seemed to be the fulfillment of an extraordinary dream Stephanie had had the morning before—she weeping heart-broken at Baba's feet, while Baba looked utterly pleased with Himself, as if He'd just done the best thing in the world.

Alex came to me a day or two later in one of those extraordinary dreams—looking as he may have looked after having been thrown from his car—broken bones and scrapes. But his face was utterly shining at me. Shining! As if to say, "It's okay, Mom. It had to happen. I did good!"

In the minutes and hours after hearing Aunt Ruby say that Alex had died in a head-on car crash, I visualized the scene over and over— what was Alex's reaction when he saw the big Lincoln heading right at him? Was he afraid? Did he shout? I'd try to imagine the impact. Oh my son! Why didn't I *know* in that instant?! For a year or so, as I drove up and down Mountain Avenue, on my way between home and university classes, I had stark moments of feeling an oncoming crash. I'd shudder and reorient myself to the normal traffic scene. A story I came to tell myself was that in his previous life, Alex was responsible for the death of someone in a car crash, and that Alex's death had balanced that karma.

It's quite possible that Luella, Danielle and Dad were both listening and not listening. What they heard was us having fun—throwing out words, topping each other, laughing at all our goofiness and cleverness—creating this quirky thing all together.

What became of thirty? *Trickly*. Forty now *freckle*. Fifty was *quizzical* (another nod to French).

> Stephanie earned a Bachelor of Fine Arts at the University of Arizona and won a full scholarship for a Master of Fine Arts at the University of Illinois, then continued there for a Library Science degree. Took two good jobs in Seattle for about twenty years. She met Ahmad, from Shiraz, Iran, in Meherabad, India in 2010 and they married in Seattle in 2014.

> Alex would be fifty-five now—I can't imagine that. Perhaps he's thirty-something somewhere in the world now. Perhaps he's a Baba lover. I can hope.

Sixty—*salami*.
Seventy—*sesame*. (Were we getting hungry again?)
Eighty—*octopus*.
Ninety—*noodle*.
One hundred became *centaur*.
One thousand was *menthol*.
One million—*moolah*. For anything over a million we ended happily satisfied with *maximillion*. I wrote each number's new name in a tiny notebook, so I wouldn't forget.

I am eighty now. My life with Karl in Asheville, North Carolina is fuller than I could ever have imagined—writing stories and poems, collecting and editing true stories from around the world, which Karl publishes, adapting stories into scripts and directing them as plays. Stephanie and Ahmad now live 15 minutes south of us. I keep them and Alex in my loving prayers. Karl too.

We sat in Luella's living room with tea, juice, cookies and smiles that shone from our insides out. I still give thanks to Meher Baba and to *Pobby*, which afforded Stephanie, Alex and me such a delightful last time together. And to the blessing of not then knowing it to be so.

Our Natural State

Our natural state—
To be helpless and hopeless—
All else is nothing.

Misunderstandings

In my mid-forties I was in a graduate program in counseling. In a long-distance phone conversation with Ilse, I shared some of what I'd read about the connection between shame and anger in John Bradshaw's book, *Healing the Shame that Binds You.* There had been a great deal of trauma and abuse in our family. Ilse had told me once, "Dad started with me before I can even remember." Somehow I had been able to set boundaries with each of my parents in my early teens. I also shared with Ilse something discussed in class—the concept of 'learned helplessness.' This piqued her interest.

Before we ended our conversation, she asked me to send her the name of the book I had mentioned. I felt pleased. Some years earlier, she'd told me she was seeing a therapist. I was glad to hear that and asked what the therapist had said about our father. There was a long moment of dead silence, then she said, "I don't talk about that." Stunned, mystified—it was my turn to be silent.

Bradshaw's book was the only one I had mentioned, and as I had two copies of it, I sent her one. A week or so later I received a scathing letter from her—she was livid, telling me she knew all about the 12-Step programs, etc., etc. I was again mystified, and shocked by the intensity of her fury. Should I have sent her just the title of the book, as she'd asked? It seemed that she was unloading a ton of her understandable anger at our parents onto me.

Unwilling to take more of that, I wrote her a note, saying I needed a break from communication with her. We didn't communicate for a year. Then I wrote, "Can we have a fresh start?" Her answer was," Too little, too late."

I tried again at least twice and was rebuffed. Eventually it occurred to me that she'd wanted to know more about 'learned helplessness' and thought she'd find it in Bradshaw's book. But it wasn't there. Perhaps she felt disappointed, deceived and angry. We never sorted it out. After five years, Ilse died due to complications of rheumatoid arthritis. At the time of her death, I had what I call a non-ordinary dream—in which it felt like a real presence and connection occurred.

In this dream, my sister and I are sitting at a small distance from each other. We look at each other and make clear eye contact. I understand that she is asking me for something and I am agreeing.

It was clear she wanted me to stay in good touch with her three children. And I have. Both her sons have now passed on, but I am in weekly, warm communication with her daughter. In this there is no misunderstanding.

It rains
You shower Your Love on us
Our love blossoms

'X' Marks the Spot

Those of you who have come to Baba after He dropped His body, saw Him in your previous life.

—Eruch Jessawala from Meher Baba

After I heard this in July 1991, I was given a single room at the Pilgrim Center in Meherabad. Each room had a framed photograph of Meher Baba on the wall. Curious about which photo was in this room, I saw Baba in a fake chinchilla jacket, pointing at His alphabet board. A flash came: "*This* is

where I first saw Him!" Next thought, "Irma, you're being silly." Looking more closely, I saw Baba pointing to the 'X' on His board. "'X' *marks the spot*,"—a second flash! Now I have the idea that I saw Meher Baba on board the S.S. Bremen on May 19, 1932 at 1 P.M. at the New York dock. Who was I then? A maid on the ship? A journalist reporting on the Indian Master?

Taken

The first time I saw His face,
my own face shone in His reflection.
His gentle smile knew me through all time.
His eyes held me in His timeless time.
I knew not who or what I was,
But I was His.

When I saw His face
I knew to follow this Man
anywhere. Forever.

Fort Daulatabad—the Tunnel

In July 1991 a van load of Baba lovers visited Fort Daulatabad, where Shivaji, one of Meher Baba's minor incarnations, had once ruled. Inside the magnificent entrance doors of Fort Daulatabad I lagged behind the others, looking for a washroom, but found none. I went on to the entrance of a tunnel that led to the fortress. An Indian guide, speaking English, approached me to say he had much to tell me as we walked through the tunnel. I hesitated, remembering I was alone—all my companions had gone ahead. I had my credit card and cash in my traveller's bag. Could I defend myself if I had to? The young man noted my hesitation and said, "Don't worry. Don't worry!" That was a familiar enough phrase that I took heart and stepped into the tunnel with him. What else was there to do? Stay back and miss everything? No.

After just a few steps, the darkness became black all around. No flashlight, nothing. I couldn't see my hand in front of my face. We walked slowly in this darkness —he accustomed to it, but so strange to me. The Indian guide explained its vital feature to me—how this tunnel had been effective in defending Shivaji's fort from invading enemies. Invaders had to go through the tunnel to access the main fortress. In the tunnel, they'd come to a divide where they'd have to choose, maybe agonize over which way to go—right or left. So they chose. Perhaps half of them went one way and half the other. But both ways ended up crossing the same place ahead where there was no roof over the tunnel. Hah! There the defending soldiers were ready with vats of boiling oil to pour onto the invaders below. Oh, the screaming! The howling! The beseeching! To no avail. This was how the fort was protected from enemy marauders for decades. The only way the fort was eventually successfully taken was due to internal treachery. The guide explained all this as we walked slowly through the pitch-black tunnel, stopped when we reached the part open to the sky. Imagined echoes of agonizing, searing, panicked pain.

What struck me about this story was that the tunnel had to be traversed in order to get to the main fortress, and no matter which way invaders chose to go, they came to the place of boiling oil.

I thought about life choices we each have to make, and the results of our choices—some paths look smooth but longer, others are rough but shorter. God's goal is always waiting for us, no matter which choice we make, all according to our karma. There is no getting around that.

Baba, Our Invisible Constant Companion

In Mandali Hall, Eruch would occasionally say, "Did you ever see that movie, "Harvey"? There a man has a very good friend, a giant rabbit who is invisible, who is always with him. Baba is like that. You don't see Him, but He is always your Constant Companion. When you are back in the United States, you should see that movie."

Early in 1992, we bought a video of "Harvey". Karl and I watched it again. This time I was struck by the childlike trust that the main character had, not just in Harvey, but in all his fellow human beings. Elwood P. Dowd was never suspicious, never said "no" to requests or demands, always saw light and good in the actions of others. He was willing to please his sister at the risk of possible harm to himself. Yet harm never came to him.

I decided to show "Harvey" to my counseling clients in an Inner Child group setting at The Haven, a women's residential treatment center, where I worked. Before starting the video, I asked them to pay attention to how Elwood P. Dowd dealt with requests, demands, situations, people, with life itself. As the story unfolded, the women warmed up to it, laughing at all the right moments.

The following week, we gathered together again to discuss Elwood, Harvey, his family and friends. Many questions came up. Was Elwood just an alcoholic, hallucinating a very large rabbit? Was Elwood codependent because he took so much care to please others, even at possible cost to himself? Did Elwood care what others thought of him? Of Harvey? What was the relationship between Elwood and Harvey? What was it about Elwood that made it possible for him to see Harvey, while others didn't? Just what kind of person was Elwood P. Dowd?

With the first question, five women started to talk at once, including the intern, an Episcopal priest. We used a pencil to function as a 'talking stick', so only the person holding it was allowed to speak. So a line formed and a discussion that lasted an hour and a half started.

"Elwood doesn't take life so seriously."

"He doesn't take attitudes when people don't agree with him."

"He is accepting of every person and situation he encounters."

"It's okay for others to have their feelings and desires."

"Elwood sees the positive side of every person and every situation."

"He makes his own reality."

"He sees the world and everyone in it as harmless, kind and pleasant."

"He is willing to go along with others' plans and wishes, not thinking of possible harm to him."

"Elwood doesn't care what others think of him."

"He is innocent, not naïve."

"No one can take advantage of him because he gives freely."

"He is what he is."

"Harvey is his best friend. They love and respect each other. They don't take advantage of each other, or make demands on each other."

"Elwood doesn't need Harvey to be with him all the time—he knows he always has Harvey's love."

"Elwood is not codependent because he does things freely without fear and only to please others, not to gain their favor, acceptance or approval."

"Harvey is not just a hallucination of Elwood's, since his sister and the doctor see Harvey also."

"Elwood believes in Harvey. Elwood believes in and trusts himself. Love and trust make it possible for him to see Harvey and to have this great relationship with him."

"I wish I had someone like Harvey."

Harvey and Elwood stayed in our minds and hearts for some time, as evidenced by continuing stray remarks. We also talked to our friends and families about them. In this way the group members received a perhaps indirect experience of Meher Baba's Love. In this way, Baba manifested as the invisible Friend of us all.

How like Baba to plant a loving seed through Eruch in Mandali Hall, and how loving of Baba to nurture the glow of this seed, inspiring us each to share its light with others. How compassionate of Baba to allow each of us to receive His gifts of Love in such a natural, warm and humorous way.

When I think of You
smiling deep into my eyes,
all thinking stops.

October, 1996

I am not in Meher Baba's Samadhi, or in His bedroom in Meherazad, nor in the Lagoon Cabin, or in Meher Abode in Myrtle Beach.

I am standing in a dirt parking lot across the road from the Bombay International Airport. Nancy Wall and I have just arrived from Tucson.

Nancy is discussing something with the van driver who will take us to Meherabad, as he loads our bags into the van.

A young Indian man is trying to convince me to pay him for putting his hand on my duffel bag as I toted it from the airport to the parking lot.

It is late. It is dark. We've just travelled for thirty-six hours—my third pilgrimage to India in fifteen years.

Suddenly
then and there
Baba speaks within me

So now you are coming to Me?

Yes

And you will be Mine?

Yes

Forever.

Yes

And I will take care of you.

Yes

Don't worry. I will take care of everything.

Yes

What is beautiful
is You alive within me.
O Meher Baba!

Surprised!

I was so surprised, not when the phone rang one day early in May 2000, nor that it was Nancy calling, but when she said, "Are you sitting down? I have some news for you." I sat down on a dining room chair in some suspense. "You have won the Martindale!" she said almost triumphantly—she was my friend and I called her my writing godmother for encouraging me. Amazement tingled through my whole being! This story had been my final project for my first writing class ever the previous fall—Beginning Fiction. Except my story wasn't fiction — I'd just changed the names.

I couldn't stay sitting down—I got up and walked to the bay window that looked out on the roses all along the patio wall. Just outside the wall, the mesquite trees heavy with catkins. Restless, I walked over to the bay window in the living room, as Nancy told me I couldn't tell anyone except Karl until the Thursday opening night of the Pima College Writer's Conference, when the winners would be announced, just before Memorial weekend. I gazed beyond the wooden gate and mesquites to the Catalina Mountains shimmering in the distance, an ocean of blue sky in between. My short story, "The Human Touch: A Triptych" had won the Martindale Literary Award for the year 2000!

I did quietly tell my friend and fellow writer, Judith, and she came with Karl and me to the Opening Night. Wearing a new red velvet jacket, I approached a large round table, where several of the hot writers in the advanced fiction class were sitting. They had invited me for drinks after our final class that week and I'd gone with them for the first time. They'd talked about who would win first prize, second and third—I wasn't on their lists. During a moment's lull in the chitchat about who would win, I said, "I'll be the dark horse." The silence lasted another moment, till Sheryl said, "I'll be the dark horse." As if I hadn't said a word.

There were a few empty chairs at their table as I approached on Thursday, but they told me they were all spoken for. So Karl, Judith and I sat at a nearby table. When Meg Files announced me as the first prize winner of the Martindale, I walked past their table keeping my eyes on Meg, then on Karl and Judith on my way back. The next day at the Writer's Conference, people lined up asking to read my winning story. Frank Gaspar, who had judged the entries, told me my story really wanted to be a book. I told him I didn't know how to do that.

Fourteen years later, I'd written up my memory of receiving the news from Nancy, and read it to the Gifts of Age writing group, which she facilitated. I was utterly dumbfounded when Nancy said, "Well, that's your version of how I told you. What really happened was that I told you in the coffee shop at Campbell and Grant." "I've only been in there once," I said, "and that wasn't with you." She stuck to her story and I didn't want to make a fuss in front of the other women there, who loved and respected her. If it had ever come up again, I would have said to Nancy, "I'm sure you told several women they'd won the Martindale in that coffee shop, but I'm the only one who heard it from you sitting in my dining room, gazing out the bay windows."

Amaging Grace

Laugh lines, worry lines—
etched signs of having arrived.
Thrilled to be sixty.

The Embrace

Charles Haynes was the guest speaker at the Southern California *Sahavas* in 2015. He said he was eight when he first met Meher Baba in the Lagoon Cabin at the Meher Spiritual Center in Myrtle Beach. He said he stayed as close to Baba as he could in the days following, and Baba always responded to his presence with a glance, a smile, caressing Charles' cheek or stroking his hair. Charles assumed this was in the natural order of things—this faithful, loving connection between Baba and himself.

One morning, Charles stationed himself as usual along the path where Baba would pass. As Baba walked by Charles, He gave no glance, no intimation of awareness that Charles stood there. Heart-shocked with disbelief, Charles watched Baba step past. With no forethought, Charles lunged and caught Baba's jacket. Instantly, Baba turned, bent, embraced Charles, face to face.

An eternal moment. An embrace lasting forever.

Charles fell silent. We took in the photo up on the screen.

The importance of attending this *sahavas* dawned on me gradually. Though I had seen and heard Charles speak at several Southern California *Sahavases* and in Meherazad, India, I never had a conversation with him. I first greeted him at the Meherana *Sahavas* in 2014.

At lunch on the second day of this *sahavas* in Los Angeles, Charles and his husband, Chris, joined our table. I contributed a few sentences about our pilgrimage to Assisi in 2014. In the afternoon open mike program, I read three poems from my book, *The Well of Longing*.

In the afternoon of the third day, we were all saying goodbye. I waited my turn to present myself to Charles. All I could say to him was, "Thank you, thank you, Baba!" as I looked into his shining eyes. Charles said he liked the poems I'd read, and we embraced.

As I prepared to release him, he grasped me more firmly, his arms wrapped all around me. He held me, and held me. And just as I always felt Baba's Love coming through Charles as he spoke of his intimate moments with Him, I now felt Baba's Love in this embrace. And I knew *this* to be Baba's embrace.

I knew now, *this* was what I'd come for.

I say Your Name—
complaints and resentments fade.
I sing Your Name—
my heart aligns with Love.

Two Chairs

I see them from half a block away, silhouetted in the Tucson moonlight—two chairs—silent invitation set at the curb, side by side. I lengthen my stride. When I reach them, I can tell they are in good shape, solid wooden chairs —lightweight with cane seats and backs. I sit on one and then the other—there in the dark. Settle into the slight give in them. Comfortable, not rickety or damaged. They'd be perfect as extras for the dining room table. Maybe I could carry the chairs home on the way back. Two blocks. But are they really here for the taking?

I back away from the chairs, continue my way to Wild Oats. My shadow stretches before me, ten feet long, my short straight hair outlined like that of a cutout doll. A swath of icicle lights glitter from the eaves of several house on the block. Reds and blues twine around mesquite and palo verde trunks. A trio of saguaros wink yellowredgreenblue. The season's fantasy blazing around me in these last days of the twentieth century.

Old Friend Orion, the Hunter, floats majestic in the eastern sky—Ancient Avatar. Sirius, the Dog Star, faithful at his feet. And God within—Meher Baba, demanding such honesty—stealing my heart, making me want to please Him. Yet desire for the chairs nags at me like ringing in the ears as I head for the side entrance of Wild Oats Market. As do the qualms about just taking them.

I don't remember wanting things until I was five years old, staying with my parents in Uncle John's farmhouse in Saskatchewan. Immigrants from Germany. In the closets I found my cousins' old scribbled coloring books, bits of crayons, *Dick and Jane* readers. But it was the Eaton's catalog that made my eyes go wide—kids with red and blue balls, skip ropes, puzzles, tricycles—toys I'd never seen before—and I wanted them. These desires followed me hot to Windsor, Ontario after we'd spent one winter in Saskatchewan. In the city I played games with other kids for the first time—sometimes with their toys too. I wanted their toys. Once I almost stole a toy shovel, but realized everyone would know it wasn't mine.

Now in Tucson, in my second marriage, in my mid-fifties, I enter Wild Oats knowing I can buy just about anything I want here. No need for unfulfilled desires. No need for just taking things.

"Do what you want, Irma. Just don't get caught," Dad said to me quietly years ago when he found me going through his pockets looking for loose change. He understood need. I'd been smoking for about a year, since I was fourteen—to stunt my growth, I joked—but I rarely had the twenty-seven cents for my own pack of menthol Cameos. Usually I'd mooch off of Ilse, five years older than me, and working, or I'd lift one of Dad's home-rolled off the kitchen window sill—but they were dry and hurt my throat.

What counted in our family was to look good. That was tough to do when it felt like I was already five inches taller than any kid my age, tougher on funds from babysitting at fifty cents an hour, and a dollar a week allowance for being Mom's house and yard lackey. The money never stretched far enough, so I took Dad's message in earnest and began to refine my skills.

I'd stuff a cotton blouse under the waistband of my skirt or undies in a dressing room, and bit by bit smuggle clothes and accessories from Hudson's bargain basement in Detroit across the border into Windsor. I got good at smiling past Canadian Customs.

It was my right to take something because I was poor. Because I wanted it. Because everyone else already had it. Because I could. Only from the big stores, never the little ones. Robin Hood's ethics.

At Wild Oats I pick out whole wheat bread, cream, English Breakfast tea. A chocolate muffin. I am grateful for the lack of piped in carols, for the muted holiday décor. Without thinking, I take two vanilla cookies from the sample tray. Eat one, slip one into my pocket. Put a box of them into my cart.

My petty thieving started with sticky-fingered snatching of three-for-a-penny blackballs at the corner store's open candy counter when I was six. I'd have a nickel to spend or maybe just three cents. With a nickel I could get a Coffee Crisp, but with three cents, I was stuck with either one toffee or nine blackballs. Heart pounding and ears getting hot as soon as the idea came into my head to just take some. This idea didn't let go of me, so when no one was watching, mouth dry and throat tickly, I slipped penny candy into my dress pocket. I'd keep a wary eye on Mary, the bleached blonde cashier, in case she'd notice something, but she never did. She'd crack her gum, admire her long red nails and take my three cents for the toffee I put on the counter. As soon as I was out the door and past the store window, I'd stuff the blackballs all in my mouth, take the long way home through the cemetery to cool down and let the evidence disappear.

"Do you qualify for our senior discount?" The young cashier, a poinsettia tucked into her blonde ponytail, speaks with a slight Slavic accent. The discount is tempting given their prices—I shake my head, smile my regret. Pull a ten from an inside pocket to pay. I step through the sliding doors into Tucson's balmy December night.

"Would you step this way, please?"

Twenty-two years ago, a week before Christmas, a man with thinning hair, hefty under his rumpled tan suit, invited me to one side of the sliding doors outside the

Safeway on Lincoln Boulevard in Venice. I glanced at the badge he held up and pushed my cart to the side. I wouldn't have known a real badge from a fake one, but I believed him.

"I must ask you to let me see what is in your bag."

I handed it over and watched him pull out the jar of freeze-dried coffee, a can of salmon and a large Ghirardelli hazelnut chocolate bar. No receipt. I was under arrest. I'd been careless. Stupid. The worst thing was that my daughter was with me. I'd never imagined exposing her to this. Eleven years old, she watched, silent and frozen. In the back of the store, the detective had me stand straddled as he patted me down. Took my fingerprints. I didn't know what to do with the black grease smudging my hands. He left to check my priors as we sat on two metal folding chairs in the dim cavernous space and watched stock boys rushing past in and out of the swinging doors. I felt sick about exposing her to this.

Take a lesson from this—don't steal." I told her. I wasn't going to be like my father. "I don't," she told me back, looking me in the eye. That made sense, I thought. She hadn't grown up wanting things the way I had.

They found nothing else on me, so they let me go. "Don't come back into Safeway," the detective said as he escorted us to the automatic doors.

I appeared in court two weeks later. Found two other shoplifters to joke with, bolstered my bravado, pled *nolo contendere* and paid the $60 fine. I was chagrined at having been caught, but I was too stubborn to take my advice to my daughter. I determined not to let this queer my skills—I resolved not to get caught again. Two days later I paid for a bra, then slipped purple cotton bikini undies into the Lowell's bag and walked out.

Early in January I applied for an ESL teaching position in Hawthorne, California. When they fingerprinted me in the application process downtown L.A., my gut told me this wasn't good. It took them two weeks to match my prints to the police record—then the Hawthorne principal called.

"I got a call from downtown," he said. "They told me to tell you not to come back into the classroom. But they wouldn't say why. Can you clear this up? I want you to stay—the people in the class really like you."

"I'll see what I can do," I said. He was a nice man and I thought I should try. I called the superintendent's office and explained I'd taken food because I was unemployed. Which was true. I almost said I wouldn't do it again, but I wasn't ready to go that far. "Mr. Farley at Hawthorne said he really wants me to come back." They didn't care.

"Try in seven years. Your record will have cleared by then." I figured it was just too un-American to risk letting me teach English to Hispanic immigrants. Yet it was a relief not to have to drive forty-five minutes through fifty-seven traffic lights to Hawthorne and back four evenings a week. I was burned out on teaching ESL anyway.

A year later I had a job as recreation director at Hirschhorn Manor, a board and care home housed in a former apartment complex on Pico Boulevard in Santa Monica. I helped Bill, the cook, serve lunches and dinners to the residents from behind the counter. He called the place a halfway house, but it was halfway to nowhere because the residents either died, sometimes spectacularly, or got a van back to Camarillo, the state mental hospital near Sacramento. Most stayed on, medicated into the thorazine shuffle, and added their cache of quirks to the daily routines of the residents and staff.

A few residents would hang out with me in the O.T. shop—a converted three-car garage off the alley behind the complex. They told me their stories as they spun around in the green barber's chair just inside the door. I wasn't trained to do occupational therapy, except for having been a single Mom with two kids, so we putzed with paper, paste and paints. Some came on the weekly trips to the movies, the mall, the museums, the beach. Others came just for the food—pretzels, chips and Kool-Aid on the monthly Las Vegas Nights, when Joe, the maintenance guy hosted Black Jack and other card games in the O.T. shop.

Irene came just once.

"Can I have an egg, Irma?"

"Not yet, Irene. We're going to color them first.

Flopped on the raggedy tweed sofa, I was amazed to see Irene step over the doorsill for the first time. Bill had boiled three hundred eggs, two per resident, for their Easter breakfast tomorrow. My heart was still kicking up a storm after carrying two five-gallon pots of eggs down from the kitchen to the O.T. shop. I watched her shuffle across the cement floor. She was old and squat, blackheads dotted all over her face. Stiff white hair stuck straight up from her head. Bed hair.

"But I want an egg now." Plaintive.

She stood in front of me in her dingy flowered duster and dilapidated mules. If I gave her an egg now, she'd still demand two tomorrow. "You'll get two with your breakfast tomorrow, Irene. You'll have to wait." I took a couple of deep breaths and pinned my hair back out of my face.

"I'm hungry for an egg now, Irma. Can't you give me just one?" Urgent.

What was going on with her? She'd had lunch. The snack bar was open. I didn't get it. "Not now, Irene. If I find any broken ones I'll let you know."

My fingers stroked the soothing blue velvet of an old cushion. My heart hadn't calmed down yet and I was nettled by Irene's insistence. Just to get away from her I got up to start the dying project.

"Can you look now, Irma? Are there any broken ones?" Irene set herself down on the sofa.

"Not yet."

Irene left after a while. Feeling a bit shaky again, I went to rest on the sofa and noticed the cushion was missing. Midnight blue velvet with a satin fringe. I'd found it on a disintegrating rattan chair—giveaways set out on Wavecrest in Venice. It wasn't exactly a treasure, but I enjoyed its luxurious blue plush. "What happened to the velvet pillow from the sofa?"

"Irene walked out with it," a resident said.

"How could she…?" I winced at a sharp stab of rage in my head. Who does she think she is? Just come in and demand an egg…then take my pillow…I felt ripped off… how dare she just walk in and take what she wants!

It hit me—a jolt of ice water.

That's what I did. What I'd done for years—just go in and take something. Because I wanted it. Because I could.

The rage subsided, sucked out by returning cortical reason. Left me shallow and shaken. I took a long slow breath…heart pummeling my chest… hammering in my head. Memory shots of my childhood, becoming aware of my parents' hypocrisy. Hating it. Hating them.

I began to stop stealing.

At first I thought it was a simple thing to know what was stealing and what wasn't—the laws of Moses were obvious. I stopped taking things that didn't belong to me. But I found myself poking through and sorting out other laws. Family laws had depended on Mom's mood, or whether Dad had work. Street laws were edgy, cool in the shadows of dusk. Tricky laws blowing like leafy branches in the wind. When had I settled so densely into the law of gross entitlement?

Might is Right. Bismarck's law had marched through the twentieth century. My parents brought it along with feather bedding in the wooden trunk Dad made before we left refugee life on a Bavarian farm. We crossed the choppy Atlantic, settled in Windsor, into the law of survival, which said that waste was worse than sin. The law of doing what you must. Our family had survived the Second World War in Germany, but bits of niceties, legalities had frozen off, disappeared like neighbors in the night, burned to a fine gray ash. When did they start doing things with their left hands that their right hands agreed not to see?

Months after the Irene incident, the day Reagan was voted president, I was ticketed for walking across a red light in Venice—a ten-foot street no bigger than an alley. A motorcycle cop, bristling leather and hard plastic, barked at me to stop. I knew I'd better smile and pay up—so honesty got to be a trip of its own. Once I trekked back to ABCO to pay for a broken carnation I'd snuck out the day before. The manager took my fifty cents and looked at me surprised, "This is very unusual," he said. I nodded and walked away, feeling squeaky clean. But when subtle dishonesties winked at me, I sometimes still winked back.

A banana moon is edging toward the west as I turn south on Jones, crunching on the second vanilla cookie. Will the chairs still be there? What if they are meant for someone else? Then they wouldn't be set out on the curb. I shift the plastic grocery bag from my left hand to my right. Headlights swoop behind me, light up the chairs ahead. There on the curb still. Heartbeat quickens, breath shallow. In a moment I'm running my hands over the varnished wood, the joints, the cane, feeling for blemishes—reasons to reject them. I sit on one chair again. Let my feet swing. Butter-vanilla lingering on my tongue.

I pick up the two chairs, one in each hand, the low backs wedged up in my armpits and continue south on Jones, slower now. Headlights confront me as I turn east on Second Street. I don't freeze, kept walking.

In the morning, I wipe the chairs down with fragrant lemon oil, welcome them into our home. I set one under an oak-framed watercolor of prickly pear in the dining room, the other by the mission oak desk.

My daughter comes to visit for a week after Christmas. I show her the chairs, tell her my story. "They fit right in," she says. She gives me a long look and we smile.

In the world of forms
there's a right and a wrong.

In the world of Love
there's only a song.

Front-Ended

"My money back!" is what I should have said to her after my trusted mechanic, Rick, told me my 1996 Camry had been front ended. He also said the state it was in, it couldn't have passed the annual inspection. I spent $600 just to be able to get it to pass inspection. It was my fault. I should have brought the car to Rick before I bought it. It looked okay to me—well, what do I know about cars. I just wanted another reliable Camry.

I called the woman I'd bought it from, told her the car had been front-ended and what it had cost to pass inspection. She was dumbfounded! She didn't sound like she was faking, but what did I know? She stuck to her story that she'd bought it from a guy who sold rental cars. Said she didn't know it had been front-ended. That was a real issue—Rick told me that once a car has been front-ended it's never really good and solid again. He ought to know—he was the best mechanic. The woman was chagrinned, telling me she was sorry, that she was a good Christian. I mostly believed her…and yet…

A year later, she called me again, out of the blue, and asked how the Camry was. "I sold it," I said. "I have a new Honda Element now." "Oh. I want to give you that $600 now. I've been feeling so bad about the Camry and my finances are straightened out now." I was silent. Amazed… remembering she'd said she was a good

Christian. She asked for my address and how to spell my name—sent me a check for $600. Karma complete for her.

I'd sold the Camry after Rick had fixed it up, to a young Malaysian man, a student—he'd be in Tucson for two years, then return home. I trusted the Camry to be reliable for at least that long, and sold it without a worry on that account. But I was withholding information that he and his buddies probably didn't know to ask for. I talked to Baba about this, told Him everything, said I'd accept anything He saw fit to do to balance my karma. Asked for guidance. Sold the Camry for a reasonable price—less than I'd paid for it. Never heard from the young man again.

It came back on me one night at Irene and Dina's way out in the desert. They didn't tell me they'd closed off a part of their driveway and at night I couldn't tell. It meant I had to back up the Element in the total darkness for several yards before I could turn around. The next day I saw sizable dents on the driver's rear side, where I'd scraped into mesquite or Palo Verde branches, fumbling around in the pitch-black night. It cost $400 to fix the dents. I figured then that I'd paid whatever karmic debt was due on the Camry.

Sudden Change

In the summer of 2015, Karl and I looked at each other and we both said, "We have to leave Tucson." We'd lived in our beautiful, private foothills home for eleven years and thought we'd live there for the rest of our lives. But it was clear now we would leave not just our lovely home, but all of Tucson. "Where will we go?" Karl asked. "Asheville," I said. A few days later Karl said, "What about Eugene, Oregon?" "Okay," I said. "Let's go look at it." We'd talked about taking a West Coast road trip for a while—this seemed like good timing.

So why did we have to leave Tucson? The first inkling went back a few years, when a woman in the therapy group I facilitated kept worrying about Tucson's water situation. I filed that concern in the back of my mind. We had a pool in the backyard—a lot of water to pay for. The final thing, the kicker, was when our accountant told us we'd only get two years off our fifteen-year mortgage by paying one extra house payment each year, not five years, as the bank representative had said. This meant I'd have to work until I was seventy-eight. I wasn't yet burned out on being a therapist, but I could see it on the horizon. Karl was already burned out in his part-time job as a creative specialist at the too noisy Apple Store.

We took our West Coast road trip in mid-October 2015— confirmed that Eugene had some excellent qualities and yet was not for us. We stopped to see the redwoods in northern California—my second and probably last time. I said Baba's prayers as I stood in this cathedral of giant trees, my voice breaking at times with awe. We visited Betty Lowman in Oregon, Marnie and Doug Frank in Portland and Stephanie and Ahmad in Seattle—looked once more at Eugene on our way back—nope, not for us. We agreed to take a look at Asheville.

For years, I'd heard from Baba lovers that this one or that one lived in Asheville, and that this one and that one had moved to Asheville. Friends who were not Baba lovers visited friends and family in Asheville and came back with glowing reports. In November of 2015, we stayed with former Tucson residents, Ken and Debby Blackman, for a week, meeting Western North Carolina Baba lovers, going to their meetings, riding around with a real estate agent, looking at possible houses.

We didn't see anything possible, but intuitively decided to move to Asheville. The larger Baba community there felt inviting. No matter how lovely our Tucson home was, it wasn't enough to keep us there—we had come to the end of our creative outlets. We sold our house, set off across the country with our beloved cat, Sasha, stayed in Susan Paul's basement walkout apartment for almost three months, bought a manufactured house, refurbished it and moved in. Our retirement cottage!

People asked us why we moved. We gave them the obvious answers, including my idea that we'd been among the Native people in the 1830s who had been driven out of their homes and force-marched to Oklahoma on The Trail of Tears. Now, along with others, we were coming back to our ancestral home—safe now—they couldn't make us leave because they couldn't recognize us.

Slowly, I became aware of a deeper reason why we left. It had to do with the three pilgrimages we'd taken with other Baba lovers: in 2010 we travelled all over India with Don Stevens and the Beads-on-One–String group; in 2013 we were on the Heartland pilgrimage with Jill English and more Beads-on-One-String Baba lovers, following Baba's tracks on the Trail of Tears from Charlotte, North Carolina to Prague, Oklahoma and back to Myrtle Beach, South Carolina; in 2014 we went on the Four Pillar pilgrimage in Italy and Spain—a much smaller group, but still with enough of the painful entanglements, agreements and disagreements that seem to mark such pilgrimages. All opportunities for personal growth.

In the course of each of these pilgrimages, we changed in imperceptible ways. Richard Budd, from Scotland explained it after our Heartland pilgrimage. When the fifteen of us met in Charlotte, NC, we each embodied a particular 'cable' of energy. As we travelled across the country in two vans, as we stopped to meet Cherokee or Black people, to say the Prayer of Repentance, to sing "Amazing Grace" in English and in Cherokee, as we paid respects at sacred places, as we conversed, ate and slept—our cables connected with each other, more deeply with some than with others—merged, blended, melded till there was one large cable travelling across the country. In this process we underwent subtle internal changes. Some of us more aware of these than others. This was what I came to see as our real work—to add our cable of prayers and songs and good will to the cable of Love laid down by Meher Baba in 1952—to widen and reinforce it so others may more easily follow it. A cable primarily of repentance, of forgiveness, of love.

So as Karl and I arrived home in Tucson after the Four Pillar pilgrimage, we were not the same as when we had left some weeks earlier. While this was true after each of these three distinctive pilgrimages, we were not yet aware of these internal shifts. It took the news of a financial burden which we were not willing to carry, for us to know it was time to move. To leave Tucson forever, though we would always love Tucson.

Baba had already planted the seed of Asheville in my mind over the years. Here we met many Baba lovers new to us and reconnected with ones we'd met before. Asheville and its surrounds afforded us the opportunity to expand our activities, to use and improve our talents in service to Baba—Karl with music, book publishing and graphic skills; me with writing, compiling and editing Baba stories, adapting Eruch's stories into scripts and directing them as plays. Our lives expanded as we used our talents to serve the community. A new and richer venue for our spiritual growth. One more pilgrimage.

A Sign

Karl and I were negotiating conditions of sale of our house with a young couple on the first day of spring, also Nowruz, the Persian New Year. We worried that the appraisal would be too low for the couple to be able to get a big enough loan—big enough to give us the funds we needed to buy a house outright in Asheville.

Karl prayed and asked Meher Baba to help us sell our house and find a suitable one in Asheville, NC.

I prayed and said to Baba that I utterly trusted that all was in His Hands, and that all that happened would be for our highest good. There was a moment when I thought about asking for a sign.

That evening I completed a project of editing photos in my iPhoto file. When I was finished I was surprised to see that my screen-saver photo had changed. The very sweet photo of our cat, Sasha, was gone. In its place was a photo taken by a Baba lover in Meherabad, India of Meher Baba's face in the clouds, above the so-called Obedience Trail, which led from the Meher Pilgrim Retreat to His Samadhi.

This trail is one of two that leads from the Retreat to the Samadhi, and is the longer one, an actual gravel path, lined by whitewashed stones and lit at night by tall lampposts. The other trail is shorter, cut across a farmer's field, thus private property, and we are not supposed to walk across it. But many, if not most of us do. We call it the Disobedience Trail.

I showed Karl the new screen-saver, and asked how that could have happened. Karl, the Apple Creative Specialist, took a hard look at the situation, and said he had no idea.

Maybe it's a sign, I said. *It must be a sign. He's watching over us. He's telling us to walk on the Obedience Trail.*

It all worked out: the appraisal acknowledged the singular aspects of our home and environment; the couple followed through on purchasing our home; we found a very suitable retirement cottage in Asheville, complete with the woods behind it that I'd kept seeing as we packed up in Tucson. Thank You, Baba!

Love runs through His veins
while we nurse our hurts and sighs
Love runs through His veins.

Lighting Up

At dusk and into the darkness of a June night, I watch fireflies light up for a second and disappear—and light up again a few seconds later a few feet away. Sometimes it's still light enough that I see their unlit bodies after they've lit up. Karl jokes that he'd like to light up like that, but he doesn't know which muscle to twitch—an old "Calvin and Hobbes" joke we enjoy. I stand on the front porch, gazing into the darkness, awaiting the brief flashes of light in our yard and in the neighbors' yards. The sparks of light feel magical, otherworldly, delightful.

A thought comes—a memory of a moment when I was fifteen years old—alone in bed, hoping to fall asleep, when suddenly I was in a different state of consciousness. In this state I was aware only of *knowing* I am not this body. I am not this identity of Irma—whatever I am, it is something else.

I don't know how long I was in this state. When I returned to normal consciousness, all I wanted was to go back into the other—but of course, I didn't know how.

The next morning I was abuzz to tell someone of this amazing experience, but I had no words to tell it and no one to tell it to.

Sixty years later, I read in *Lord Meher* that one morning in November 1958, Meher Baba rose and told Bhau, His nightwatchman, that He'd stayed awake all night, thinking of each of His lovers.

It was in November 1958 when I experienced that amazing state of consciousness. I now believe that Meher Baba thought of me in that moment…that in that moment, He lit up my consciousness and let me know I really am something beyond Irma. Like a firefly lighting on and off, I came into and out of that consciousness. I have never forgotten the *knowing*.

How many nights

I came out to gaze
at the bottomless sky
intent to see a sign
coursing through its stars,
wanting, still wanting
something to guide me,
reassure me of what
my heart already knows—
All is well.
All is well.

April 6, 2021, I am driving north in the left lane of I-26, headed toward a chiropractic appointment north of Asheville. I am driving about 65 miles per hour as I approach a gentle rise in the road. I reach the top, and suddenly see the car ahead is almost stopped at a short distance from me. There is, in fact, a long line of vehicles creeping up ahead. I brake hard. Immediately! But the distance is too short—I will crash into the car ahead. Or fishtail if I brake harder and slide into either or both lanes beside me. Lose control of the car.

In a split second I see a short open space between the car ahead and the one coming up behind on my right. In the second I see it, without thought, I swerve into the right lane. As I do that, I'm aware that I could smash into one or both of those cars. But I don't. I swerve and zip cleanly through and drive on.

My heart beating fast. Mind half stopped. Half wondering if the other two drivers think I'm some kind of hot-dog driver. No matter. I drive on. The traffic picks up speed ahead.

Suddenly, it is clear to me that it was Baba who directed this swerve! Baba saved not just me, but several people and vehicles. If I had crashed into the car ahead, it would have crashed into the one in front of it, and that one too could have crashed, and on and on. Or if I'd hit one of the two cars as I swerved, that too could have caused further crashes.

I keep replaying that instant of choice, that instant of action—the immediate follow through. My one chance... and I just took it!

It may be that Baba in this way lightened some heavy karma for me with this instantaneous swerve. His Love, His Grace threading me through maya, as He as done all my life.

More and more,
it feels like Now.

Where Are You From?

When I'm asked here in Asheville now, I say Tucson, because I came here from there and I'd lived in Tucson for thirty-three years. It now feels like my hometown. But I wasn't born there and I didn't grow up there. I was born in Krenau, Germany in 1943, but I didn't live there—it just had the nearest hospital in Silesia for my mother to give birth to me. Besides, after the war that area became Poland again and the city's name was changed.

So I'm not from there. My parents weren't from Silesia either—they were from what is now Romania, which had been the Austro-Hungarian Empire before WW I. And I'm not from there. My first memories from ages two to four are of Witzelsdorf, a village in Bavaria, where we lived as refugees—so I'm not from there either.

I was five when we arrived in Windsor, where I grew up. Grade school, high school, university—it used to be my hometown, but there have been too many places since then and I no longer feel that I'm from there. My parents and I emigrated to the United States in 1962. I stayed in Windsor for university, but married Cliff Sheppard, an American. I lived in Mount Clemens for two years and in Ferndale for ten—had two children and then a divorce. Three memorable years in Venice Beach, and though that is where I came to Meher Baba, the most life-changing event ever—I can never claim to be California girl. After a year of international travel and wandering, I certainly was no longer from Ferndale. A year in Norfolk, Virginia, homeschooling Pagan and teaching English to Saudi women—not long enough for me to be from there.

Then Tucson—the Sonoran desert is the greenest desert on Earth. Karl and I married in our lovely backyard. I earned a graduate degree and worked as a psychotherapist—over twenty years in private practice, mostly in a home office. We lived in five different homes, ending up in the foothills of the Catalina Mountains—we thought we'd live there for the rest of our lives...I will always love Tucson...and yet I am not really from there, not a native, as they call it.

Where are you from? What does that question mean? What do they want to know? Where are your people from? Where did you grow up? What was your last place of residence? If I feel I'm not from any of these places, them where am I from? Responses people do not expect to hear are: I come from my parents. I come from God. I come from my last life on Earth. I lived here two hundred years ago, before it was called Asheville, and now I've come back. So I don't say those things. Perhaps it's a matter of responding with whatever I most identify with...

I've just turned eighty and I'm in my eighth year in Asheville, so quite a newcomer. I may live here for the rest of my life. When I go to the Meher Spiritual Center in Myrtle Beach and someone asks me where I'm from, I say Asheville.

Home can only Be
within my own heart beating
in time with True Hearts.

Epiphany

There is only Now
There is only You